T0246045

Street
Hearts

An Extraordinary Story of
Saving Street Dogs

Street
Hearts

EMMA and ANTHONY SMITH
with LISA CUTTS

Harper
North

HarperNorth
Windmill Green
24 Mount Street
Manchester M2 3NX

A division of
HarperCollins*Publishers*
1 London Bridge Street
London SE1 9GF

www.harpercollins.co.uk

HarperCollins*Publishers*
Macken House, 39/40 Mayor Street Upper
Dublin 1, D01 C9W8

First published by HarperNorth in 2024

1 3 5 7 9 10 8 6 4 2

Emma Smith, Anthony Smith and Lisa Cutts assert the
moral right to be identified as the authors of this work

A catalogue record for this book is
available from the British Library

HB ISBN 978-0-00-870194-9

Printed and bound in the UK using 100%
renewable electricity at CPI Group (UK) Ltd

In loving memory of Jane Duberley

Contents

Foreword

by Kate Lamb

'How are *you* the one who didn't get bit?' Emma exclaimed, as we closed the crate doors on two feisty puppies who had just made very clear and concise arguments as to why they really should be left to fend for themselves on the road in a small village in rural Bulgaria. Luckily for them, we didn't completely agree.

This was my first morning out 'dog catching' with Emma and her husband Anthony. I'd arrived less than ten hours earlier, deposited in darkness at the bottom of the bumpy road leading to their property at 2 a.m. and then 'four by foured' up to a chorus of barking dogs and the promise of a soft bed.

It was the winter of 2016. I had just finished my last season in *Call the Midwife* a few months before and then, quite unexpectedly, had to put down my long-time companion, Willow the chocolate Lab, days before Christmas. And so, jobless and dogless and just a little bit lost, I sought out the things I knew made me happy – snow, friends and dogs. I ride-shared my way across France to snowboard and dogsled, and then headed onwards to

Austria for more mountain-based happiness-seeking, before finally convincing some Yorkshire expats in Bulgaria to let me continue eastwards and help them look after some dogs. They were stand-offish at first, but I was fairly insistent, as my Facebook Messenger history reminds me.

Over the next two weeks I would work alongside them and learn about how this couple had found their dreams of pastoral bliss in the Bulgarian mountains somehow hijacked by dogs. So many dogs!

To say I was inspired by them is an understatement. I could see how much they cared for the dogs they saved but also how they could do more – hopefully without bankrupting themselves in the process! Emma and Anthony had converted their wood-sheds and outhouses into makeshift kennels and were paying for vet bills and food for forty dogs, eventually renting out their guest bungalow to some rock-climbing friends of mine to miti-gate the costs.

I channelled my energy into training the bitey puppies from day one, setting up a computer admin system, a rolling online fundraiser and generally being a bit 'too helpful'. I found myself completely unable to resist the couple's endless Northern prac-ticality and the real sense of achievement you could get after a day outside getting covered in muddy paw prints.

At Street Hearts there's always a problem to solve and always some way you can do more. While that can seem overwhelming at times – witnessing suffering and cruelty always takes its toll on the heart – when a dog you first found shaking with fear runs up to you wagging its tail and asking for love, it's hard to deny how important their work is.

That summer, I adopted Scout from them and cycled her from Bulgaria to London to raise the funds that would enable Street Hearts to run as a licensed shelter. All these years on I couldn't be prouder of what they've achieved and what they continue to do for their local area, all their adopters and the dogs they've rehabilitated and rehomed. I'm over the moon that their story is being told now.

I've never met anyone like Emma and Anthony. Every single day they expose themselves to heartache, physical and emotional labour, threats from people who want to stop them, dogs who want to bite them and red tape that risks their entire operation. And they still keep going, with humour, grace and that Northern practicality. They're some of the best people I have ever known, and I'm delighted you can now get to know them and some of the dogs they've rescued.

Kate Lamb, 2024

Lessons in Avoiding Dog Bites

Emma – Then – 2015

Anthony and I fell in love with Bulgaria very easily. The culture and calm way of life were unlike anywhere else we had been, so it didn't take long for us to decide we wanted to build a life here. And it's fortunate we found so much to like about this country and its inhabitants, otherwise we wouldn't be able to bear situations like this one.

When the call came from the local mayor, the Bulgarian voice on the other end of the line had told me that the dog was huge and angry – not the best news. Still, we wasted no time in setting off. Our descent from mountainside into the valley and back up the other side, our battered blue Toyota bouncing around in clouds of dust, was like something out of *The Dukes of Hazzard*. Our enjoyment of the unspoilt Bulgarian hillside was somewhat lessened by the impending sense of permanent maiming. As we pulled to a stop, I readied myself to leap from the vehicle, desperate to get between the dilapidated shed where the snarling dog was holed up and the farmer who had got it into his head that banging a stick on the walls was a helpful thing to do.

I hit the ground running, yelling at the man to get out of the way. A look of momentary surprise crossed his lined face as he realised that not only was an English woman speaking Bulgarian, but she had the audacity to tell him what to do. You can take the woman out of the police force, but you can't take the *it's-best-you-do-what-I-tell-you* out of the woman. It's all part of my enviable skill set. Anthony, meanwhile, headed to the back of our pickup to get the capture kit. I'll grant you that it's not a name that translates well to the uninitiated in calming and rescuing street dogs, but it's a necessity in our line of work. Our rescuing days were in their infancy at this point, meaning our equipment was somewhat on the basic side. We learnt fast: pain really focuses the mind.

I repeated my instructions to the gawping farmer and he reluctantly moved aside, but not before he told me how I should approach the problem. This was a village we knew well: it had an elderly population with outdated views on animal welfare, and yet every property owner had a dog. Sadly, I didn't rate any of the dogs' chances of longevity. Anthony and I rushed over here at the local mayor's request, aware he wouldn't have called us if it wasn't necessary and urgent. The pitiful story was that two local brothers had got drunk and, stumbling home in this small, remote village, decided they would torment a dog to pass the time between oblivion and sobriety. Of course it had retaliated and bitten one of them on the leg and the other on the arm, earning it a kicking. And here it was locked in the shed. Their master plan had been to leave the dog to starve to death. Fortunately, the local mayor got to hear about it and, being a compassionate man and animal lover, he called us. So, not for the first time, and not for the last, we were ready to try and save the dog.

The mayor's request had been to have the dog neutered and return it to the village. But as we stood next to the shed, the sun relentlessly beating down, the hound threw itself again and again at the flimsy door, and Anthony and I exchanged a look. We knew that what he was asking was impossible. Even if we managed to get the dog out without it seeking its revenge on the gathering spectators, these people would undoubtedly kill it later. We absolutely would not let that happen. There is always the flicker of a chance that any dog – even one as unstable as this dog – can be rehabilitated. Sadly, the same could not be said for the two sorry siblings responsible. We weren't there to redeem their souls, but to rescue the dog.

Whatever the dog had endured, it was certainly not going without a fight. Do we get scared at times like this? Yes, but I didn't doubt for a second that we were anywhere as close to being as petrified as the dog. I scanned the dirt track and nearby crumbling buildings and took in the scene: one of the men who reportedly caused this horrendous situation was keeping his distance. I watched him peek out from behind a gate, a wailing woman, apparently his wife, clamped to his side. Good for them: they managed to secure themselves behind a solid object while Anthony and I dealt with the fall-out.

'We're not bringing the dog back here,' Anthony said to the mayor. 'If we take him, he's not coming back. We'll decide what happens to the dog.' I love and admire his no-nonsense attitude, especially as it echoed my own thoughts. 'We'll get the cage from the truck and see how it goes.' Both Anthony and I knew that the mayor wouldn't argue. He wasn't really in a position to do so, and besides, he always supported us and didn't think twice about tearing into those who abuse and neglect their animals. Many Bulgarians want to see an end to animal cruelty, while sadly, many, like the inhabitants of this village, didn't think that killing an animal past its best was wrong in any way.

By now, we had drawn a crowd, mostly watching from a safe distance and paying more attention than they ever would have to a dying dog whimpering and howling as its life ebbed away. I helped Anthony unload the cage and as we set it down, there was the distinct sound of splintering wood as the dog repeatedly rammed itself against the door. A huge brown eye appeared in one of the ever-growing gaps and locked on to me. Quite how life took me from North Yorkshire police officer to being stared down by a raging mountain dog in the Bulgarian countryside, I failed to recall at this moment.

As Anthony opened the cage door, I ran an eye over the amassing crowd. It was a force of habit after years of policing, coupled with a concern that someone here might decide to take things into their own hands. A quick recce assured me there was nothing that looked like a firearm. I could momentarily relax. As far as you can with a snarling dog inches from your face, anyway. Was his aggression beyond the point of no return? This was clearly not the time to ponder that particular worry.

I grabbed a packet of dog food and tore it open, squeezing the contents into a metal bowl. 'I bet the dog hasn't had a drink in who knows how long?' I said to Anthony as I moved back out of the way, steeling myself for the dog's release. I squinted up at the cloudless sky, failing to remember when it last rained. A number of Bulgarians feed their dogs the occasional slice of bread but water is not always a consideration.

I wiped my hands on my overalls, glad that I left my fleece on the backseat of the Toyota on such a warm spring day, yet wondering why I thought bare arms was a smart move against sharp canine teeth. One more eye over the villagers and I nodded at Anthony to signal that I was ready. Whatever was about to happen, I hoped that the dog was so hungry it went for the food rather than for us.

Adrenaline flooded my system as I waited for Anthony to open the door. He bided his time and waited until the dog was away from the door. I knew what he was thinking: he didn't want to upset the dog any more than necessary, as well as giving it time to adjust to the daylight flooding into his holding cell.

Gingerly, Anthony opened the shed door as I held my breath. From my position 8 feet or so from the open door, I heard the kind of snarling that made the hairs on the back of my neck stand up. Between me and the cornered animal was a four-foot-high metal cage, a packet of Winalot chunks and my husband of less than four years. I love all animals – I'm clearly referring to the dog here and not Anthony – but I couldn't help thinking that this was going to go one of two ways.

With an almost eerie calm, a black nose on a long white snout appeared in the glaring sunlight. As the dog edged its way through the gap, I couldn't stop myself from staring into its huge brown eyes. The dog's massive brown and white head was topped with large, pointed ears and the curling lips accentuated a fair set of teeth. I braced myself for a malnourished twenty-five-kilo dog launching itself at me, aware out of the corner of my eye that Anthony was doing the same. However, as the mammoth animal warily made its way towards the cage, I remembered that it was probably more scared of us than we were of it.

Sure enough, the dog's lips uncurled and his nose twitched as the smell of food reached him. He took a tentative step in the direction of the cage and, with the briefest of hesitation, walked into the cage straight towards the food. I dropped to my knees beside the dog as he gobbled down the food and said, 'It's OK, Big Lad. You're safe now.'

'Go on then,' said Anthony, as his boots came into view beside me. 'Say it.'

I put a hand up to shield my eyes from the sunlight, looked up at him and said, 'Teamwork makes the dream work.'

'I'm glad you're so positive,' said Anthony. 'Now we need to put our fingers through the metal grating and lift the cage into the back of the Toyota. And Big Lad still looks hungry.'

'Well, you go first then,' I said and slowly stood up, the dog taking no notice of me now that he had some food for the first time in two days.

I got ready to pick up one end while Anthony did the same at the other. Neither of us fancied waiting for the dog to finish his food, and he was making short work of it. I gave a silent hasty prayer that Big Lad wasn't about to barge his way out. He would have little problem reaching my throat that was a little over 5 feet from the ground if he launched himself at me.

At last, the cage and dog safely in the Toyota, we were making tracks to our home about 30 km from the village. Anthony took his time on the roads, both of us aware that the cargo was not best pleased with the day's progress. Whenever we stopped at a junction or roundabout, I listened out for signs that Big Lad was settling down. There was a good chance that this was his first outing by car. At least it kept him quiet. The cage was secured, but the downside of being a former police officer is the constant risk assessment of each and every scenario.

Exhausted but elated that we had the dog safely in our care, Anthony drove up the last leg of the journey, taking his time navigating the steep one kilometre stone track that led to our home in Glushka village in the beautiful Dryanovo region. Anthony parked the Toyota in its usual spot – at the top of the track between the gate to our own property and a neighbour's house. The six-foot-high wooden gate in the stone wall opens on to our garden – what was left of it – a bungalow and our house.

I rushed through the gate and across the courtyard to our outside summer kitchen, ignoring the views of the Stara Planina mountains, focused instead on picking up some gardening gloves. They would be better than no protection from Big Lad's teeth as we manoeuvred the cage from the pickup. We carried the cage to one of the sheds across from our house. We knew that it wasn't the best place to put him: he was about to move from one shed to another, so there was little in the way of progression. 'We can't let him out before we're certain,' I said, as much to myself as Anthony.

Big Lad's behaviour had been terrifying, and now he was watching us as he constantly moved around the little space he had in the cage. With some seventeen other dogs spread over our 20 acres of land, Big Lad needed to spend some time on his own before we could let him out. He'd been so tormented by food –

starved and teased with it – that he was constantly growling and snarling, with no sign that it was going to stop. The only way that I could feed him was to push food through the metal grating towards him.

While Anthony spread some straw on the concrete floor and filled up a large metal water bowl, I took my time sat on my haunches in front of Big Lad, easing the food to where he could get it without feeling threatened by me. He took a small piece and then moved over to the far side of the cage, back to growling. He then edged forward and took another piece, again and again. He was so scared; it was unpleasant to watch.

'Let me know when you're ready, Anthony, and I'll let him out.'

'Leave it. I'll deal with him, you get clear.'

I stood up and wiped the dirt from my overalls. 'Gallant offer, except I know that you're only looking out for my welfare because it's my turn to get the tea on.'

'Correct,' said Anthony, a true Yorkshireman of few words. He emptied another packet of dog food into a different bowl and set it down a few feet from the cage, his every movement tracked by Big Lad.

'You'd be lost without me,' I said as I stepped back towards the sunlit courtyard, making sure I was well clear of the door.

'For a bit,' came the reply. 'Housekeepers are inexpensive in this part of the world.'

'I'm not beyond shutting you in there with that dog, you know.'

Anthony sighed, safe in the knowledge that I'd never do anything of the sort, and I listened for the sounds of a dog about to have a meal for the second time in as many days.

8

Now, Big Lad warily stepped out of the cage, heading straight for the bowl of food. We watched him in companionable silence for a few seconds until we closed and secured the shed door.

Would our new addition come back from the brink? Anthony and I were ready to do whatever it took, but sadly, even our best sometimes wasn't enough. For now, we had another seventeen dogs to attend to.

2.

Raising Livestock to Saving Dogs' Lives

Anthony – Then – 2015

Every morning started with Emma and me waking up and one of us asking the other, 'Is it time for bed yet?' We love Bulgaria and the life we've made for ourselves here, although I would freely admit that we weren't prepared for the shock of seeing so many abandoned and unwanted dogs roaming the streets. We were trying our best to stop the problem, despite the frequent thoughts that there was only so much that we could achieve. Still, one dog at a time. Today was the day that we started to work with Big Lad and find out if we could actually help him.

I'd lived in Bulgaria, on and off, since 2004, although it wasn't until June 2013 that Emma and I moved into our house in Glushka. Before then, we had spent a small fortune renting a house in England and we knew that our money would go so much further here. We had left the UK with a vanload of possessions to become the proud owners of a new house with plenty of land, all for a price of £56,000. I've been so fortunate to have had such a wonderful life, brilliant upbringing and a variety of careers. But I think it's safe to say that everything I'd experienced in my past had led to the life we have now.

Growing up, my family wasn't wealthy, but we had everything we needed. My dad was a Yorkshire farmer, as was his dad, and I helped run the family farm in my early life. My dad's dad was one of eleven children, my dad one of five, and I was one of four. I had the most amazing, hardworking parents and thinking back never fails to summon blissful thoughts and happy memories, of haymaking in summer with my dad, mucking in with help from neighbours to get the work done. We'd order crates and crates of Dandelion and Burdock. I can vividly recall the van rattling up the lane with the glass bottles knocking against the metal crate, and there was always one waiting for us when we were done.

I remember long hot summers, my parents having two farms in West Yorkshire at the time. One was in Wilsden and the other Cullingworth. It was always fun, and Christmases were great with second hand Scalextric sets and hand-me-downs. This was a different time and a very happy one with fabulous parents. They were great people and brought me up with honesty and taught me integrity.

I think this upbringing left me pretty grounded about matters, and Emma probably is the same now too. Although she'll probably tell you that I've worn her down with my personality. She's hilarious like that. But in all seriousness, Emma and I have both tackled problems with the same attitude. And one of our shared principles is thinking about animals and their feelings.

My wonderful dad sold the independent farm he owned in 1999, and that was the end of farming for him. I was totally devastated when he passed away in April 2022. His death had a huge impact on me; it had a huge impact on all of us.

Being a farmer was obviously a colossal part of my life, and it gave me a deep understanding of animals. I suppose it will sound strange, even contradictory, but I had compassion for the animals we bred and took to slaughter. When we started to rescue street dogs in Bulgaria, the haunted look in the petrified dogs' eyes was one I recognised. It never occurred to me as a child that seeing animals go off to slaughter or even watching them being slaughtered was in any way an abnormal thing to watch. Most people don't think about the animals when they're killed for meat, or in fact, probably don't want to think about it at all. Even the transportation of live animals has nothing humane about it. When we moved to Bulgaria, I made the decision to become a vegetarian, prompted by the realisation that if dogs felt petrified at the thought of being taken to a safe location and looked after, how much terror goes through an animal's mind as it's being taken to its death? Those thoughts never leave me.

My sister's family are still farmers and we stayed with them after my dad passed away in spring a couple of years ago. My dad was buried on my sister's farm in May 2022. The spot where he's buried overlooks the land my parents farmed when we were children. Despite the sadness of the occasion – we all miss him so much we spent a beautiful spring evening talking about him and saying our goodbyes together. No one feels my dad's absence as much as my mum. My incredible parents have always supported me, and that's all I can do for my mum now. Apart from tell her that she's the best mum ever and I love her very much. I hear other people talk of parental disputes and disagreements. I'm blessed that I've only had love and encouragement from my mum and dad.

As we sat outside on my sister's farm on the day we buried him, with the day drawing to a close and the children playing in the garden, the cows in the field next to us came over to the dry-stone wall that separated us from them. My sister commented that their behaviour was interesting, but to me it was clear they wanted to be a part of what we were doing. My view of animals has had a seismic shift since we came to live in Bulgaria.

It was these thoughts that accompanied me as I walked across the courtyard to the shed to see how Big Lad had fared overnight. Today was the day we would find out if we could actually help him.

I suggested to Emma that I took one for the team and entered Big Lad's new domain on my own. She didn't argue. I opened the door and took my time. He first moved away against the far wall, still growling, but making no attempt to come near me. I started to chat to him as I went about sweeping out the soiled straw, filling up his water bowl and dropping some pieces of dry food into his bowl. Hunger overcame Big Lad's apprehension and he inched forward, had a quick swipe at the food and moved away again. As I took my time cleaning out the shed, he moved backwards and forwards to his bowl, each time taking a tiny amount of food, snarling continuously.

It was clear that it would take some time before this dog would be ready to join the pack running around in the sunshine outside. We'd only lived here a couple of years; so much of the surrounding land around the house was unfenced, meaning the dogs came and went as they pleased. What would we do with Big Lad if he couldn't turn a corner? We had no way of rehoming dogs, so it was a problem we would face when the time came. Our best hope was that he adapted to life here and lived out his days with us. He couldn't go back to the village and we couldn't release him on to the street.

Whatever happened to Big Lad, we had done the right thing. Every dog we take in, or have neutered, prevents potentially hundreds of other unwanted dogs, although we've barely made a dent in the problem.

We had come a long way since the night we turned up to our new home in the pitch black, no food and our belongings stuck somewhere on our trailer at the bottom of the hill. I had said to Emma at the time, as we inched up the hill in the dark to our front gates, that we would work it out – we always did, together.

3.

I Couldn't Point to Bulgaria on a Map

Emma – Then – 2015

I watched Anthony through the glass partition in the kitchen's double doors. He was on his way across the courtyard to check on Big Lad. The dog hadn't shown many signs of improving. After several days, the routine hadn't varied: one of us would put some food down, he'd growl, take a tiny amount, sit down and growl at us again. Meanwhile, ten of our other dogs were making a nuisance of themselves as they rushed around my feet, desperate for attention and full of energy even with the morning walk. Despite its challenges, I wouldn't change this life for anything. It was my idea to do this, after all.

It felt like a lifetime ago that we'd arrived on the threshold of our new home, absolutely clueless as to what Bulgaria had in store for us. Before I met Anthony, I wasn't even sure where Bulgaria was and probably couldn't have pointed to it on a map. Even so, my current situation – in Dryanovo surrounded by dogs – was one I wouldn't change for anything. Anthony and I often have the conversation about how we ended up here, on some sort of crusade to help every street dog we encountered. I'd had a number of changes of direction in my life before we came here, but I'd say that every major part of my past had led me here. Certainly, those experiences have affected how I tackle any challenge that comes my way now. And believe me, life at times throws up enough of them. I'd never blamed Anthony for finding myself at the emotional raw edge of man's incredible cruelty to animals, nor finding myself constantly trying to stem the tide of abandoned dogs. I blame myself.

I grew up in the late seventies and early eighties in West Yorkshire – in Yeadon and then in Otley. When I was eleven, we moved to a place called Oakworth, where we lived practically next door to the train station where *The Railway Children* was shot. I was brought up by my stepmum and dad along with my two stepbrothers. I didn't have an easy childhood: sadly, my biological mum had serious mental health issues, which left us estranged for twenty-five years. Such problems can be hereditary, and schizophrenia in particular runs on the maternal side. Part of what drives me is that I know I could one day face the same difficulties in life that so many of my family have endured, including my mum.. Perhaps that's why I chose a career first in nursing and then in policing, or why I invest so much time and energy into helping street dogs. I consider myself extremely fortunate. When I finally got in touch with my mum after all that time, I realised that my love of animals came from her. My caring, compassionate side came from my mum.

My dad is a self-made businessman whose drive and ambition had such a positive impact on me. He has done so well for himself and I know his enthusiasm for achieving positive outcomes was something that he instilled in me. Both of my parents have contributed in their different ways to enable Anthony and me to be successful today.

After I left school, nursing seemed like a very worthwhile career. If not an easy choice, I knew it would stand me in good stead for the rest of my life. So, in 1996, I began a four-year degree in nursing. The first year was tough going and I failed my exams. It was a bit of a wake-up call so, never one to back away and admit defeat, I learnt to apply myself academically, to study properly and effectively, and quite simply, I sat down and put the effort in. From then on, I got through the exams easily. My first nursing job was in a large Yorkshire teaching hospital, where I forged some strong friendships, not to mention made some memories.

Quite soon, I met a student nurse, Jocelyn, who was studying at York University. She came to work as a student on the Medical Admissions Unit where I was based. We became good friends and had a lot of fun. We were nurses in our early twenties and were pretty much left to get on with it. Nothing I do now could ever compare to those night shifts. One night, Jocelyn and I were working together on a twenty-six bed mixed Nightingale ward along with another nurse, Tara, and Annie, the Sister. In the space of a single shift, a man haemorrhaged so badly it splattered the ceiling, while the machine for warm blood transfusions repeatedly broke. A lovely man who had leukaemia needed the transfusions, but due to the malfunction, I wasted a ridiculous amount of time waiting for the antiquated thing to reset itself. Someone else was withdrawing from alcohol and ran straight through a glass door. Another man experiencing withdrawal symptoms monkey-poled down the ward, swinging from the curtain rails. To calm him down, I thought it would be a good idea to get him a corned beef sandwich and finally, after much persuasion, he stopped behaving like a primate and got into bed with his sandwich. I drew the curtain around him but when I went back to check on him the sight was enough to put anyone off corned beef sandwiches for life.

After that absurd night, I developed the best friendship with Joc (pronounced Joss). We had each other's back, regularly worked together and shared the same dark humour. Two years or so later, Joc moved down to London – in search of better cheese and wine, she joked. It was typical of her to be impulsive, even if the driving force was a cheeseboard.

By 2008, Joc was travelling the world, but then she became unwell. It took some time to get to the bottom of what was wrong with her, but she eventually shared the devasting news that she had been diagnosed with cervical cancer. She lived another three and a half years post diagnosis. I did everything I could for her, both emotionally and practically, but my amazing friend had limited time left.

I got together with Anthony in 2009 and spent a lot of time sitting with Joc, talking to her about Anthony. He lived in Bulgaria, I told her, and I wasn't entirely sure whether I should join him out there. She said, 'Why don't you just try it? What's the worst that could happen?' And that simple question has always stuck with me. When I took Anthony to see Joc, the second he left the room, and despite her weakened state, she leaned across to me and said, 'Marry him. He's definitely the one for you. He's really nice.' It was one of the last things she ever said and I'm grateful to have that lasting memory of her wise words.

Joc died before Anthony and I were married in September 2012. Her death really knocked me for six. She was young, beautiful, with a cracking sense of humour. We had banter and a lot of fun together. And she was really the reason I moved here. Since losing a friend at such a young age of a truly horrible, horrible cruel disease, I thought why not embrace all that life has to offer? Life is for living, not regretting what you didn't do.

4.

Dream Big, Aim High

Anthony – Now

I've set the day aside to repair the fence alongside the boundary to the puppy run. Emma comes with me to supervise – I wouldn't have it any other way – but she's soon distracted by one of the thousands of other tasks we must take care of every day. Street Hearts has evolved into something that neither of us could have predicted. We've managed to rehome hundreds of dogs and paid for thousands of neutering operations. At this point, we have seventy dogs waiting for adoption. Keep up though; it's ever-changing.

Our house and the bungalow aren't entirely unrecognisable from day one, but the rest of the place has gone through a transformation. We now have 20 acres of land, and when our neighbour's house across the track went up for sale, we bought that too. It wasn't an easy decision, yet the risk of hunters buying it was a prospect that chilled us to the bone. We've separated the house into a two-bedroom ground-floor apartment where our volunteers stay, while the apartment upstairs is where our full-time member of staff, Lucy (Lyudmila) Krumova, lives.

I grab some of the tools I need from the workshop above the staff kitchen, leaving Emma to let the adult dogs out of their living spaces. Other than the puppies, every sociable adult dog, plus a few of the unsociable ones, gets the option of a morning pack walk with all the others. These walks seem to have become our USP – they're what every volunteer, visitor and member of staff looks forward to doing and seems to be the most mem-orable thing everyone takes away with them. A walk with sixty or seventy dogs is a pretty decent way to start the day, although I don't always get time to go. Besides, it's Emma the dogs follow and stay with on the walks. I have my favourite dogs, and the dogs have their favourite human. It's the natural order of things.

Some minutes later, I'm up to my elbows in dirt and all sorts of unsavouries when Emma and Lucy, plus around seventy dogs, pass by. Tipsy, a grey and white mixed husky with mismatched eyes, gives me the briefest of sniffs and then runs off to join the pack, closely followed by Big Lad. Some are making much more noise than others, including Emma who's busy whistling at the ones who are already straggling before they've even left our prop-erty. They always find their way back.

Little Blackie, the smallest adult dog at Street Hearts, decides that she's going to keep me company as I mend the fence. Now, she's definitely *my* dog, there's no doubt about that. She stands about 25 cm tall, weighs 8 kg and I'd guess she's about eight years old. Most evenings she finds her way onto my lap, although I could hold her in one hand.

Back in 2017, Julian Petkov who owns the local petrol station called me to let me know that there was a little black dog running around near his property, and initially, he thought that the dog had puppies with her. Emma and I took him a cage and said that if she turned up again, he should pop her in the cage and we'd collect her. And sure enough we did. Emma calls Little Blackie a rat – I think she's jealous.

When we went to get Little Blackie, she had milk, but we couldn't find any evidence of puppies. We didn't know whether the puppies survived or whether she had given birth only to be abandoned by her owner. Wouldn't it be incredible if the dogs could tell us their stories? Or would it be too distressing?

The day starts better than I anticipated: the fence needs to be reattached to the post which is simple enough to do and takes me a lot less time than I'd expected. Little Blackie shimmies her approval at me, and then finds something much more interesting to occupy her morning when she realises that I'm about to start clearing up after her ninety-nine housemates.

Broom in one hand, industrial sized poop-scoop in the other, I decide that I may as well start where I am by the puppy runs. I pause for a moment, marvel at the solitude that being six hundred metres above sea level brings with it, and breathe in the clean, crisp air. I love the forest at this time of year, especially the morning birdsong.

The walkie-talkie attached to my belt crackles into life. 'Anthony,' says Emma. 'Have you fixed that fence yet?'

'Oh, for f—. I've done it. What is it now?'

'In that case, can you get on with clearing up the mess and sorting out the dogs' medication. It's Lauren's day off today.'

'I know it's Lauren's day off,' I say. 'She told us at breakfast. I'm capable of remembering what happened an hour ago.'

'If you're in one of those moods, I'll get on with the walk.'

'You do that, and possibly leave me in peace.'

I go back to appreciating the sounds of nature in our corner of the Bulgarian countryside, and then tackle the clear-up. So many dogs, so much mess.

I walk from the metal gate that signals the start of the pack walk, make my way in front of the runs, back towards the gravelled communal areas. The shelter has seen so many improvements over time; I have to stand and picture it without the drainage, without the hygiene and water stations and the open-sided staff kitchen where we keep the staff rota, dog food and medication. We've come a long way in the last ten years.

My twenty-four years as a commercial diver had given us personal financial security. It meant that we could buy our house and there was enough money left for us to get by. I'd spent some of my savings buying tractors and diggers to use around the place for renovation work, never dreaming that I'd be using them to dig irrigation ditches for water pipes and clearing the ground for dog runs. I also bought a van which, at the time, I didn't realise would come in very handy for transporting large numbers of dogs to their new homes. Some of my commercial diving colleagues bought less practical items such as cars, jewellery, mountain bikes, road racing bikes, wine collections, designer gear. None of that made me happy. We were already living in Bulgaria when I called it a day on my career and, initially, Emma was at home while I was offshore. I wanted our dream home to be incredible and for us to have all the practical things we needed.

It wasn't all plain sailing: before I quit the profession, I worked for a company for 106 days, doing twelve-hour nights travelling between Norway and the Shetlands. I kept thinking about coming home to Bulgaria and regret that I didn't. Then the oil slump hit, the company I was working for went bankrupt and I never got paid. I had spent three months working for nothing, going ashore in the Shetlands in the snow (it was May). With hindsight, I should have walked away. My next job was in Kazakhstan. That job I actually did walk out on after a few weeks. I knew that it was over for me and things needed to change. Bulgaria was calling me.

It wouldn't be entirely true to say that we 'accidentally' opened a dog shelter, although it was never the plan. Neither of us thought that our initial idea in 2015 of fundraising for street dog neutering was going to lead to a full-scale rehoming and rescue shelter. Today our work involves regular transportation runs across the continent with twenty newly adopted dogs on their way to a better life in the UK. We've adapted and grown with the challenge, and what a challenge it's been.

As I stand on our land, relishing the space, dotted with happy, healthy dogs running up and down the pathways, our chickens clucking away beside our two rescue pigs, I'm proud of everything Emma and I have achieved.

5

We Were Only Supposed to Neuter a Few Dogs

Emma – Now

I'm well aware of the annoyance in Anthony's voice and can picture him moaning that the walkie-talkies aren't meant for checking up on him – they're for emergencies and safety. It doesn't stop me smiling as I tuck the handset back in my pocket, my attention now on the dogs and my surroundings.

We've climbed several more metres uphill, the farmhouse and outbuildings some distance behind us. Once through the forest and bracken, most of the dogs race backwards and forwards across the enormous open field. One or two remain by my side: I think I'm a strong leader and the dogs do tend to stay with me. I don't completely understand why they do, but the beauty of dogs is that they love people and need the guidance that humans give them. It's what makes them so loyal. And it's what makes my life so phenomenal.

My story before moving out here involved a lot of tough situations and challenges that I willingly met head on. Nursing and policing gave me an insight into the best and worst of people, but before witnessing the scale and severity of the street dog problem here in Bulgaria, perhaps I had only caught a glimpse of human failings. The dogs aren't the issue, it's the people.

I had known Anthony for several years before our friendship became anything like a relationship, and I was aware he spent a lot of his time living in Bulgaria, a country I knew little about. During that time, I went about my life, and he went about his. As things slowly developed between us, we saw more and more of each other until we were officially a couple and planning our future together.

One day he said, 'Shall we buy a house in Bulgaria?' I'd already visited for a holiday and seen its beauty and loved the simplicity of the lifestyle it could offer me – or so I'd thought. Property was very cheap in comparison to the UK too. For four years Anthony and I rented a house in England prior to us making the move, so financially, it made a lot of sense. It took another three years of visits to Bulgaria before we found the right home – and here we are, in the village of Glushka, our very being defined by dogs.

I can't deny that I found it difficult at first after I moved out here, the pace of life being so different. I'd spent the summer of 2012 on public order patrol in London for the Olympics; by September of that year, I was married. In January 2013, I was on a career break from the police – it's going very well, thanks for asking – and within five months, I was arriving in the dead of night to move to a house I hadn't set eyes on. Anthony had said words to the effect of, 'I've seen the house for us,' and I'd replied, 'I trust you: buy it.' My friend Joc's attitude of living life to the full spurring me on. I had always been a busy person and worked shifts since I was seventeen years old. And as I rattled around in our new beautiful Bulgarian home, Lottie my border collie for company, Anthony often working overseas, I wondered frequently what normal people did in the evenings. I don't watch much television, or read more than the occasional book, so what was I supposed to actually *do*? At the age of thirty-nine, I knew that I was far too young to retire. But it turned out the answer was there all along.

The first inadvertent step towards our new life started one evening in May 2015. Anthony and I made a perfectly legal, yet clandestine, visit to the local tip. We had some garden furniture we had cleared from our house and thought it better to do it late at night. While we wanted someone else to make use of it, we didn't want people to see us disposing of it, their perception being that these foreigners were throwing away perfectly good furniture. It seemed like the least insulting way of passing our unwanted belongings along was to get rid of them in the dark, leaving them to one side where someone could easily retrieve them.

As we started to unload the furniture, we heard a noise in the undergrowth. We froze, unsure what was crawling through the scrubland towards us. There are plenty of jackals in the area, but they don't tend to drag themselves forwards on their bellies and poke their heads out amongst the leaves. Then, the most mangy, pitiful-looking creature I had ever seen – up until that point, anyway – crawled out from beneath the scrub and branches, creeping ever closer to me. This pathetic animal inched nearer and, as I reached out, she licked my outstretched hand.

Any outing by car, no matter where it was, was always well stocked with a bag of dog food in case we came across hungry dogs, this late-night tip trip being no exception. I stayed with the forlorn dog while Anthony went to get some kibble from the back of the truck. He scattered some on the ground and we watched her devour it. All I could work out about the animal was that she was female, black, and there was no way we could leave her here. We picked her up, put her in the truck, and named our very first rescue Tipsy.

We drove home, minus the furniture, plus a dog. It didn't take much persuasion to get her into what was then a ramshackle potting shed to the side of the summer kitchen, now a clinic. We bedded her down for the night and wondered how she was going to be the next day.

In the cold light of day, Tipsy was a total mess, covered in oil with fur matted black. She was, in all honesty, ugly. I didn't think she would recover, but I underestimated how strong-willed she was. This beautiful husky mix with her odd eyes is proof that a dog's life can be turned around.

My collie Lottie was getting older and squabbled a lot with Tipsy, but we all rubbed along together. The most important thing about bringing Tipsy home that day was that we knew we wanted to help more dogs like her. So, the head count – not to mention the leg count – went up dramatically.

The plight of the dogs we saw on a daily basis got to us. It crawled under our skin like a parasite, and we reached a decision early on that if we couldn't ignore it, which was never an option, and we couldn't do something about it, we were left with no choice but to pack up and go home. It felt like admitting defeat and we both knew in our hearts that we had to do something. Other expats told us that neutering was the way to tackle the problem, so with this simple plan, we set the wheels in motion to arrange for a few dogs to be castrated at the local vets. What could possibly go wrong?

6.

Decisions to Make

Anthony – Then – 2015

'We've been here over two years, and we're not doing enough.' I heard Emma before she reached the bottom of our farmhouse staircase, the dogs clipping across the ceramic kitchen tiles to greet her. Tipsy took advantage of the distraction and rushed for the open dishwasher door, managing to get a few good licks in at that morning's breakfast plates, until I moved her out of the way.

I watched Emma, recognising the serious look on her face as she crossed to the kitchen table, her shoulder-length dark hair still wet from the shower. Emma sat down at one end of the wooden table; I grabbed our coffees and sat next to her.

'What should we do?'

'More,' said Emma, 'much, much more.'

'Ok.' I took a sip of my coffee and eyed her warily. My wife was one determined person when she tackled something. When I'd gone vegetarian Emma fully embraced it, learning to grow, preserve and cook entirely different foods from those we used to eat. When we moved, Emma fully immersed herself in a new way

35

of life here, but she also took intensive Bulgarian lessons, with a determination to get the grammar just right.

Emma picked up her own coffee and looked at me over the top of the mug. 'We need to speak to someone who can help us, make things official with the dog neutering programme. Remember that one of the neighbours' daughters spoke to us about a Miroslav Semov? The guy who's up for mayor in our local elections?'

'She did make him sound as if he's a forward-thinking type of person,' I said, understanding exactly where Emma was heading with this. 'And I happen to know that he'd like to meet us.'

'You kept that quiet.'

'We could really make a difference if we get his backing and official approval.' I took another sip of my coffee, felt Tipsy's paws on my thigh as she tried to get in on the conversation. 'We're in a good position to make this happen and we certainly have the time. We've already seen the dire situation with people throwing their dogs away like garbage when they've finished with them, not to mention failing to neuter them, perpetuating the problem.'

'Ah rubbish, good point,' said Emma. 'Let's invite him over and we'll talk to him about dog neutering and rubbish. It's such a beautiful country and there's litter strewn everywhere.'

'I think that we should start with the dogs.' I gave in and let Tipsy have the head-scratch she was so desperate for. 'We need a name.'

'Something catchy and memorable,' said Emma, an expression of concentration taking hold.

'We need "neutering" in there somewhere.'

'And Dryanovo.'

'How about "Dryanovo Castration Programme for Dogs and Cats"?' I said.

'Yeah, I really like that,' said Emma. 'It's catchy and something that people are bound to remember.'

A couple of weeks later, Miroslav Semov arrived on our doorstep, an air of authority around him, giving every indication that he was a man who could get things done. His presence was very noticeable as soon as he walked into the room. There was a reluctance on his part to talk in English, but as we were in his country and Emma and I could speak Bulgarian to a reasonable standard, we obliged. When he asked Emma what she would change about Bulgaria given the chance, she wasted no words. 'I'd stop people from dumping rubbish and do something to prevent so many stray dogs roaming free. The solution to the street dog problem is a neutering campaign.'

As we sat at our kitchen table and talked, it was abundantly clear that Miroslav had a different view about dogs than most Bulgarians. He told us that he had spent time in London where he had attended a course run by the Dogs Trust. 'If I'm voted in as your local mayor, I'll make sure that a neutering programme for street dogs gets off the ground,' he told us before he bade us farewell. 'You have my word.'

Once we were alone, Emma said, 'I believe he'll do it. This could be the opportunity we need to change everything for the better. Besides, Miroslav is the only candidate who made the effort to see me. He's completely won me over; I'm voting for him.'

I nodded in agreement. 'All we have to do is wait for the local elections, hope he's our new mayor, does what he promised and then gives us the legal authority to capture and neuter the dogs before we let them go again. Easy.'

'For the first time since we moved,' said Emma, 'I can see a way for us to really help these dogs.'

Both of us took a moment to watch our newly adopted four-legged friend as she ran across to jump on the sofa and make herself at home.

'It'll be a lot of work,' I said. 'There are so many street dogs, not to mention the cats. It's a lot to take on.'

'We can do it, I know that we can. What could possibly go wrong?'

7.

It's Election Time

Emma – Then – November 2015

Before Anthony and I set off into Dryanovo town centre to cast our votes for the new mayor, I made sure that Poppy, the tiny puppy we were fostering for another expat, was going to be OK while we were out. She had been found in a bin, starving and covered in ticks. When the vet examined her, Poppy had tested positive for Lyme disease and initially had to be syringe-fed. It was hard going, but we adored sweet Poppy, and she was another reminder of how many dogs needed help. I intended to remain true to my word and vote for Miroslav Semov. I chatted with Anthony about what it would mean to us if he was the new mayor and he actually did what he promised. And, more importantly, what it would mean for the local street dogs.

Our descent into the town took us along roads with dogs' snouts protruding from the shadows, litters of puppies behind rubbish bins, and some running along the road. We both knew that it would always be too much to see these starving, discarded animals who had been let down by humans.

'How long do you think it'll take us to get the street dog population under control?' said Anthony, as he slowed the Toyota, avoiding a small tan and white dog that had raced across the road in front of us.

I let out a long sigh. 'A year, two years? Or is that me being hopeful? Perhaps we never will.'

'There must be something like thirty dogs and puppies we've passed in this short journey. Not to mention the ones that repeatedly get dumped at Gesha village.'

'And the ones that get dumped by Gesha well too.'

'If we get them neutered, there's a hope it'll not only keep the numbers down,' said Anthony, 'but people won't automatically think it's OK to chuck them out like everyone else does. Perhaps people will stop blindly following everyone else's irresponsible actions.' Our conversation was always dominated by the plight of the dogs, and any lull was filled with the topic of raising money to help them.

As we pulled up outside the single-storey concrete community centre, I saw that events were well underway. There was a slow trickle of people entering and leaving by the main door, on their way to or from casting their vote.

We said hello to one or two of our neighbours, exchanged pleasantries in Bulgarian and went inside to show our ID. A rather stern-looking middle-aged woman gave each of us a ballot paper and pointed in the direction of a line of booths along the inside of the community centre's far wall. The tables, chairs and bookcases had been pushed into one corner to make way for the voting booths.

Anthony headed for one and I walked over to another, pulled

the curtain around me and examined the paper. I could speak Bulgarian to a high standard, but unfortunately, I couldn't read the Cyrillic language as well as I would have liked. I could read about subjects such as dogs with ease, but not elections and voting. It dawned on me that I wasn't actually sure where I was supposed to mark the paper. I struggled for a minute or so, trying to work out what on earth I was looking at. I started to get a bit panicky, but then realised that the problem was easily overcome – I'd get Anthony to show me where I needed to put a cross.

I stuck my head out of the curtain and called out, 'Anthony, come and help me.'

The moment he stepped inside the booth all hell broke loose within the community centre. People started to shout and someone from the ID checking station surged towards us as if we'd committed the worst atrocity ever. As I've pointed out, my oral and aural knowledge of Bulgarian was good, good enough to understand that I'd just made my vote null and void as soon as Anthony crossed the threshold of the booth. It was abundantly clear that secret ballots were taken very, very seriously, and no chance of vote influencing or intimidation was happening in Dryanovo community centre on polling day.

A little crestfallen, I left and ignored the stares of the other voters. 'That was interesting,' said Anthony as we reached the Toyota. 'Next stop, the wood yard. What can possibly go wrong there?'

'I doubt that my one vote will make all the difference anyway,' I said, as a way to lift my mood.

Anthony gave me a look and turned the pickup in the direction of Tryavna, a town about half an hour's drive away.

41

Another adjustment we'd got used to was the business of keeping warm without central heating. Our home is heated by fires, so when we moved here, we needed to find a wood yard to supply us. We were told of one on the outskirts of Tryavna and met Rumen who runs the yard. At one point, we thought of setting up a business selling furniture. We'd design it, Rumen would make it and through our Facebook page, Nutty Oak was born. We sold tables, chairs, breadboards, all through social media, mostly to friends and family. We weren't earning a great deal of money from it, but still, it funded the trips home across Europe in the van. Anthony had made a bed for me and suspended it from the roof of the van. It left space underneath for the furniture and, along with Lottie my border collie, I'd drive across Europe with a van full of furniture to deliver. While I couldn't say that I was being paid a wage from the work, it covered the cost of the trips, plus I got to go home and to keep busy.

Issues started to creep in with production problems for Nutty Oak, but rather than let people down with orders they had placed, we knew when it was time to wind down the business. Besides, rounding up street dogs and getting them neutered, along with the fundraising to support it, was going to take up a lot of our time. It all hinged on Miroslav claiming victory at the polls.

Anthony drove us on towards the yard, past a number of dogs and unwanted puppies living in and around the surrounding area leading up to the wood yard. As we got to the village of Radovtsi, we drove past a large building where a notice in English on the gates declared that beyond was the 'Centre for

People With Mental Derangements', not a sign you'd ever see in the UK. There, we saw numerous dogs running loose in the grounds. Sadly, we knew that the next time we came this way, they would still be here with no one having done anything about it.

We knew that we would encounter more stray dogs at the wood yard and then again when we headed back to Dryanovo town. It was overwhelming seeing them all left to fend for themselves, without food, shelter or anything to prevent them from having litter after litter of puppies, the circle never broken.

Not long after I'd moved out here, some friends from England came over to visit us in their camper van and we took a drive around the area. We went to the hospital grounds and I gave a tin of sardines to one of the dogs. It all but ripped my hands off to get to the food. It was so hungry that once the fish was gone, it started to eat the can. My friend Chris said to me, 'What the hell are you doing here?' His words (they were a bit more colourful than that) struck a chord with me, and I thought that I couldn't continue to live in Bulgaria and see this level of suffering. This was another moment that made me understand that Anthony and I had to do something. This was important.

'I know what you're thinking,' said Anthony as I peered through the pickup window. 'I'll put money on it. You're thinking that if Miroslav gets voted in – despite being one supporter down – he'll help us get things moving and we can start right here in the hospital grounds.'

'You know me so well,' I said. 'We're well suited, you know.'

'My mum always said that I could do better.'

'I'm ignoring that and thinking about the dogs. I can't entirely blame the hospital staff for wanting them gone either.'

'I don't suppose that the patients are too thrilled about them mating, fighting, scavenging and leaving mess outside the hospital grounds,' he said, as one of the larger dogs did just that.

'We'll start around here then, at the hospital,' said Anthony, 'just as soon as everything's legally in place with our new mayor.'

I crossed my fingers and hoped that if we couldn't remove each and every dog from the street, the very least we could do was to have them neutered. One thing at a time.

It was smiles all round when Miroslav was elected as the new mayor of Dryanovo. Only a couple of days after he took office, Anthony and I were invited to a meeting with him at the local municipality offices: an imposing concrete building opposite the town square with a set of steps leading into its recessed doors.

We gave our names at reception and waited to be escorted upstairs to the waiting area. We took a seat on the long leather bench, cautiously eyeing up the thickly padded door that led to the mayor's office. Along the upper part of the white walls ran a gallery of framed photographs of former municipality leaders and mayors. There were so many, one row of headshots had been joined by a second underneath it, stretching all the way along the walls.

We didn't have to wait long before we were taken to Miroslav's large office. We followed his secretary through the insulated double doors – a throwback to communism to ensure no listening at keyholes – and received the warmest of welcomes from Miroslav. We chatted in Bulgarian and I congratulated him on his landslide victory, although I omitted to tell him that I played no part in his win. He'll probably laugh about it one day.

With a flourish he produced a document granting Anthony and me written permission from the municipality to go out and neuter the dogs in the local area. I was only too delighted to pose for photographs next to Miroslav in front of the Bulgarian and Dryanovo flags. Anthony captured the moment on his phone so that we could proudly share our first victory on our social media pages.

I couldn't contain my glee at having the legal authority to do what Anthony and I had been building up to do for so long. I felt like tearing out of his office, rushing home and launching a plan, except there was still so much to do. We were aware that we needed help to do this, lots of it. Not to mention money. And a vet. The list was endless, but now we were more determined than ever.

8.

The Bus Stop Dog

Anthony – Then – January 2016

With the mayor having granted us authority, we were ready to go. We had been granted a modest budget of 400 leva (£200) per month from the municipality, and friends in England as well as expats in Bulgaria donated money to us for neutering. They were raising the money through boot sales, charity events, raffles, discos, anything they could think of to get some much-needed money together. It wasn't only me and Emma doing this – there are expats all over Bulgaria funding neutering of street cats and dogs and feeding the abandoned ones with money from their own pockets, plus fundraising for the animals. We knew that all we could do was to try and stem the problem of unwanted dogs in the area; there was no way that we could actually take any of these dogs in – apart from the nineteen we already had by now. Even though this wasn't going to get all of them off the streets, we had to try our utmost to do something constructive.

Emma and I set out early in the morning to start the neutering programme, having planned to head towards the mental health hospital near to Radovtsi village. After much debate, we decided that although tackling the problem of the twenty-eight dogs within the grounds needed to be started as soon as possible, we would set our sights a bit lower for our first outing. There was a bus stop a short distance from the gates of the hospital and every time we drove past, we saw a dog all on her own. She was always curled up on a coat in the corner of the bus shelter, alone, miserable, undoubtedly hungry, and shivering. We'd named her Bus Stop Dog. She was there night and day, her nose to her tail, resting on her makeshift mattress. It wouldn't surprise me if she was responsible, along with several of the other starving dogs within the hospital grounds, for a host of unwanted puppies. But her fortunes were about to change for the better.

A little food meant that we easily persuaded this gentle girl to get to her white-socked feet. She was medium-sized, and her light brown fur was covered in ticks. Her little face looked so sad as I picked her up and placed her – parasites and all – in the back of the Toyota.

'Look at her,' I said to Emma, who, like me, was feeling a bit emotional – well, as emotional as a Yorkshireman gets. 'She's officially our first patient. What shall we call her?'

'I'm not sure it's a good idea to get too attached to her,' said Emma, peering at Bus Stop Dog. 'Look at her, the poor thing.'

'Let's get her home,' I said, 'then we'll give her a name.'

'Ok, then. Agreed. But we can't keep her. Once she's neutered, we'll release her again.'

'It's a bit of bad timing,' I said as I drove us home. I had to be offshore again in a couple of days.

'I'll miss you.'

'Really?'

'Yes, there's all that work around the place that needs doing and I don't fancy driving the tractor,' said Emma.

'What makes you think I'll let you drive the tractor? Besides, have you forgotten that we've arranged for Valeri to come in and do some building work while I'm gone.'

'Listen to you being all precious about your tractor. You know what you are, don't you?' said Emma in a tone that probably meant she was joking.

'You can't call me *that* with Ellie in the back.'

'That's what we're calling her, are we?'

'It's better than Bus Stop Dog.'

A few days later, I was miles from home again. I used to enjoy the work, but I missed Emma and our home together. I'd got to know Emma way back in 2007 and because I knew that she was a police officer, I asked her to sign my passport. After that, it was another two years before we saw each other again. I was visiting my family in the UK, and I contacted Emma and asked to meet her for lunch. At the end of the meal, she said goodbye and walked away. I watched her go and thought, 'if she looks back at me, she's interested.' She didn't so much as glance over her shoulder. I wasn't convinced I'd ever see her again.

I didn't even know entirely what being a commercial diver entailed when I first saw it advertised, but I thought it would be a good way to conquer my trepidation of water. I'd tried diving once before, from a yacht in New Zealand. There were fearless young children diving into the ocean and swimming under the bow and I had been a bit envious. I'd made a bit of a mess of the dive, so I suppose I was keen to put it right.

I went to Exeter for a three-day aptitude test to see if I was up to this new career. After jumping in the docks and being submerged in the dark, I went on to a five-week intensive course in Exmouth, Devon. This was my indoctrination to a twenty-four-year long career in commercial diving, travelling the world repairing ships, oil lines, reservoirs, dams, docks, wind turbines and even diving for several TV programmes.

My diving has taken me to South America, Norway and other parts of Europe and I've travelled a great deal, taking on some interesting and diverse jobs. But none was as rewarding as the one I've ended up doing. And it basically all started with Ellie, the Bus Stop Dog.

9.

The Easy Part

Emma – Then – January 2016

Anthony's flight had left a couple of days ago and I wouldn't get to see him for some weeks. I'd got used to his periods of absence over the last two and a half years, although it didn't make it any easier. I'd got my hands full with the building work that Valeri had taken on, as well as managing our own dogs and keeping an eye on Ellie, who was recovering nicely from her operation.

That first year or two, when Anthony was working offshore a lot, I threw myself into yoga. I used to go to Veliko Tarnovo three times a week to practise yoga and meditation. We'd even had plans for a yoga retreat. Imagine how boring that would be! It would mean people too, and with people comes hassle. Dogs are much simpler. I certainly wasn't going to live in a country without learning the language, so I took Bulgarian lessons. And Nellie, Valeri's wife, taught me to garden the Bulgarian way. Due to the extreme weather and seasonal variations in availability, food is often preserved in glass jars here. If you want something, you often have to grow it and then make sure there's enough to last by making sure it's preserved correctly. Looking back, I was struggling to adjust. Quelling the street dog problem seemed like the perfect solution.

I walked out of the farmhouse to speak to Valeri to see if he needed a caffeine fix, but I was sidetracked by the mountains. I took a moment to admire the views of the snow-covered peaks in the distance. I never tire of it. Several of the dogs scampered up the steps behind me and jostled for pole position to find out what I was doing. Ellie had taken to following me around. She was clearly feeling better and her recovery had been speedy. I looked down at her sitting next to my feet, her bushy, white-tipped tail doing a good job of sweeping the stone floor as it swished back and forth.

The seven or eight dogs that had braved the weather and crossed the courtyard from the farmhouse all turned towards the high wooden gate as Valeri stepped through into the garden. Excitedly one or two ran towards him, realised he was friend not foe, then rushed off to roll in the snow. Ellie was a different matter: she raced over to his side and stared up at him, adoration in her eyes.

Over the last day or two, Ellie really seemed to have taken a shine to Valeri, and I got the impression that the feeling was mutual. He bent down to stroke the top of her head and spoke softly to her, her ears twitching in response, her tail now wagging nineteen to the dozen. I really didn't want to put her back on the streets, but we couldn't keep her. As hard as that was going to be, we simply didn't have the facilities or resources to keep every dog that we had neutered. How crazy would that have been? This wasn't some sort of shelter for dogs or a rehoming centre. I couldn't imagine the work that would entail. How would we even go about it? The dogs we had here, like Tipsy who we found at the rubbish tip, were totally our dogs and weren't going anywhere. And nineteen was quite enough. If we had been foolish enough to dream that every dog we took from the streets was a keeper, we'd fail at this long before we managed to get off the ground.

But Valeri? Was he an option for Ellie?

Anthony and I first met Valeri in 2013, not long after we moved in. Our neighbour who used to own the house across the track employed Valeri to carry out some building work. We got chatting with him, became friends with him and his wife Nellie, and, of course, saw the quality of his work. We asked him to work for us on the occasions that Anthony was away or unable to do the work himself.

Valeri and Nellie already had a dog, but it was kept on a very short chain, as is typical in Bulgaria. Each day that Valeri was here, he'd catch glimpses of Ellie as she ran free around the place, interacting with other dogs and humans. All she was doing was actually behaving like a dog. Valeri commented to me once or twice that Ellie was more intelligent than he initially gave her credit for. He got to see firsthand how much joy and companionship a dog could bring when it wasn't chained up night and day. I didn't want to talk him in to taking her, but it would be a huge weight off my mind. One less mouth to feed for us. For the time being, I decided it was best if I focused my energy elsewhere and let him complete the work, while Ellie had a chance to fully recover. What really needed my attention was our plans for the Dryanovo Castration Programme for Dogs and Cats. One thing at a time. It was less than three years since we'd moved here, and leaving so much to fate, and Anthony's judgement, really hadn't worked out so badly so far.

Valeri and Nellie decided to adopt Ellie, of course. We'd found Ellie a fantastic home. It was lovely that Valeri had spent time around Ellie and the other dogs, seen her play and chase a ball, something he hadn't witnessed a dog doing. They took her home to live in the house and gave her the run of the garden, completely grasping now that dogs shouldn't be restricted by being constantly chained up. Ellie completely changed their feelings towards dogs.

But I barely had time to celebrate this first, albeit unintentional, rehoming before the neutering programme really began to build momentum. I psyched myself up for another municipality meeting. This one was a touch more interesting and taxing than the last one. It was me, Miroslav Semov our mayor, the vet tasked with the dog problem and a local woman called Antoinetta Stavreva, who had been looking after the street dogs and feeding them. Miroslav told us about the modest budget he had to spend between the municipality and the vet. The vet seemed very sceptical: he didn't think that he would get paid for his work. That had happened before, so it was understandable. Antoinetta, who we have grown to know, loves street dogs and had been doing so much for so long. But our views were frequently at odds, so things got a little terse, to put it mildly. We both wanted the same thing – to take care of the dogs and stop the cruelty and neglect – but getting there was going to be a struggle.

With everything slotting into place, I could feel in my bones that 2016 would be the year that we really got down to work. We would make as much of a dent in the problem as we could, but I didn't think it was ever going to be enough for the scale of the issue. Every single penny was accounted for as it dwindled away, scratching at the surface of the problem, still leaving so many dogs out on the streets.

Antoinetta Stavreva, local advocate of Dryanovo's street dogs

Before Anthony and Emma arrived in Dryanovo, I was the only one taking care of the street dogs in the region. It was such a relief when they started to professionally catch the dogs and look after them – this took a lot from my shoulders. Since my arrival here in 1981, I've tried my best to help the animals and to save them with almost no funds. I've got by, collecting money from friends and neighbours to buy them food. Not everyone was happy with me feeding the dogs. There was a suggestion that I was being paid to do it, which couldn't have been further from the truth. I hid as many dogs as I could in basements, in derelict buildings and in the old cinema across the town square from where we are now in the community centre. In the early nineties, democracy was coming, meaning for the moment, the police could shoot them indiscriminately.

Things got really bad back in 2000. Dogs were being collected from all over the municipality and taken to Gabrovo shelter, where after two weeks, they would be euthanised. Along with a handful of other people, I was taking dogs off the streets and hiding them. I couldn't stand the thought of that happening to all of these dogs, who were facing such death through absolutely no fault of their own. I still get upset now when I think about it. I used my own money to travel to Gabrovo and get some of the dogs back.

The shelter in Gabrovo still exists but it's very different now, and what I've described to you, regarding euthanising the dogs after two weeks, doesn't happen.

Other than me, the people in Dryanovo who took the most care of the dogs here were Pencho Rashkov and Radka Pereva. These two – particularly Pencho Rashkov, who kept eighteen dogs in his garden in Gesha until his death – did so much to feed and keep the animals safe from the municipality. There were times it was necessary to keep the dogs on chains to stop them running away and either getting shot or poisoned by locals or getting caught by the municipality. Other times, we smuggled them out to communal derelict buildings outside of town. We used to keep them there to recover after paying a vet from Gabrovo to come and neuter them. Some of the costs for this were covered by an organisation that in turn received funding from the municipality to get as many spayed as possible. We then had permission to keep those dogs.

We've had situations where, in the run-up to local elections, dead dogs have turned up all over the streets. The rumours were that a political gain could be made by eliminating the problem prior to the voting, but I don't know about that and really could not say at all that there is any truth to it. If no one claims responsibility, then no one can claim the electoral win.

Over the years I've made numerous complaints to the police about the dogs that have been shot and poisoned. I've kept all the correspondence in binders. The answer I get is always the same: there's not enough evidence and we can't prove anything. I've written to the prosecutor in Gabrovo and get the same reply there too.

We have had money come from overseas that has also been used to help the dogs. The America for Bulgaria Foundation gave money to the American Agora Association, which in turn asked the Bulgarian people to pitch for funding in various projects. In 2011, we had a public forum in Pleven attended by different groups from the town, and I put together a pitch. We managed to secure funding of 6,000 leva. We used the money to buy a VW Caddy, put crates in it, collected dogs from the village and brought them to the vet here in town where they were neutered.

In communist times, only a few privileged people were allowed to have house pets, so perhaps that has something to do with the struggles we're facing now, as regards many people's mindset towards dogs. The door is always open here at the community centre to talk about dogs; unfortunately, not many people are interested in them. Something special will have to happen to provoke them into caring.

Our town is so lucky having Emma and Anthony right in its midst. Most districts don't have any help for their street dogs or any kind of shelter at all. I'm so happy that of all the places they could have moved to, they chose us.

10.

Monika

Anthony – Then – April 2016

In April 2016, only a few months after we established the programme as a going concern, we were asked by some people in Dryanovo if we could arrange to have their dog neutered. The answer was an unreserved yes, so we went to get her.

The process was becoming more streamlined by now. It should have been easy once we had the money. The deal was, and will always be, that if anyone wants their dog neutered, no matter who they are, Emma and I will find the money: take your own dog to the vet or we'll collect the dog and pay for the neutering. It took some time to get the right vet. We tried a couple of different ones, not without obstacles. With one of the vets we used, we came up against an issue with the stitches coming undone after the neutering procedures, meaning we had to keep the dogs with us for five days while they healed. That was unacceptable; after such a long time away from the street, the dogs then lost their place in the hierarchy, so we were setting them up to fail. After some trial and error, we were put in touch with Dimitar Dimitrov, now our trusted and admired vet.

Of course, we've had all our dogs neutered after rescuing them. For several days after Big Lad arrived here, he was still very aggressive, but he needed to be neutered. We had everything crossed that it would calm him down. It was still early days for us; we were very much tackling the unknown with him. We couldn't use food to gain Big Lad's trust because he'd been so deprived of it; it just made him bite. His domain was our front yard and to begin with, Emma simply sat with him. She didn't put any pressure on him, partly because she was a bit wary of him, but because he was the sort of dog that you couldn't push into action. He had to come to us and do it on his terms. I spent hours and hours with him – we only had seventeen other dogs when we took Big Lad in – and between the two of us, we gave him the time and space he needed. Slowly he started to come to us and to trust us.

Eventually we coaxed him out of the shed and back into the cage, put him in the truck and took him for neutering. It turned him round: he was a completely different dog when he came back. It's fair to say that it still took a few days to gain his trust. Because he was a bigger dog, the op was a bit more irritating for him. Puppies tend to be fine and get over it quickly, but dogs of Big Lad's size are made that bit more uncomfortable by it. That added to his frustration over the next few days, but when he did recover, he became a total softie of a dog. He was another reason we knew that we had to do more to protect the region's dogs. Owned dogs are particularly difficult if they've been mistreated because of their behavioural problems. Almost no one wants a vicious dog and it takes so much time to rehabilitate the dog – if it can be done. And time is a resource we never have enough of.

The mayor who helped us rescue Big Lad didn't return to politics, which was a very sad day for us. He had always helped us a lot and really gave a grilling to the people who were cruel to the dogs. They deserved it. The dogs needed more allies like him.

We knew we could never put Big Lad back on the streets and rehoming him would never be a wise option. His behaviour wasn't ever going to make that a possibility. If someone accidently trapped his tail in a gate or stepped on his foot, his initial reaction was to bite you. It was as if he then had second thoughts about what he'd done and then he would be all over you as if he was trying to apologise. I'd say he wished he hadn't bitten you, but thought, 'I've done it anyway, and I'm sorry.' Big Lad would always have a home with us and live out his days here; he would only end up getting into trouble if anyone inexperienced tried to take him on. We warned anyone who came into contact with him about his tendency to snap, and things were never an issue. In total contrast, Big Lad completely cowered if another dog had a go at him, which happened from time to time.

Emma and I left the dogs – including Big Lad – running around the yard and set out in the truck to collect the dog for neutering. The family who owned her explained that they kept her at their vegetable garden which was some distance from their apartment and they would meet us there. We bounced along in the pickup for the thirty-minute journey, having already called Dimitar and arranged the operation.

We really weren't prepared for the sight that greeted us at the vegetable garden.

'Oh, for f—' I started to say, as I pulled the Toyota over. Emma held up her hand to silence me.

'What is wrong with people?' said Emma, failing to keep the anger out of her voice. We both got out and walked towards the small stretch of land, green shoots neatly arranged in rows as the produce poked from the dry ground. Next to the final row of vegetables was one end of a very short chain secured to a wooden pole that had been banged firmly into the earth. The other was fastened to a dog's collar. The dog was near starvation. She was skin and bone with her ribs protruding through her fur and clearly wasn't being fed. This was a solid 'Oh my God' moment for us.

When we told her owners that she was too thin, they were genuinely shocked. As she was chained up, there was no escape for her from any other male street dog, resulting in an unknown number of unwanted puppies over time too. The owners allowed us to take her away to the vet to have her spayed, where he discovered that she also had a hernia. He thought that this might be the result of her pulling and straining on her collar that was chained to the ground. Mercifully, the owners agreed to her medical treatment as well as the neutering.

Dog and cat food is reasonably priced here, yet people don't always feed their animals at all or else give them bread or other unsuitable food. The wrong diet can lead to illness and frequently results in deformity, as the dog's bones can't grow and develop correctly. Not for the first time, Emma and I reflected that education was the way to stop this happening.

'What are we going to do with her?' said Emma. 'We don't really have any choice but to return her to her owners once she's been neutered and the hernia treated. At least we can make sure she eats properly and puts on some weight.'

I put her in the back of the pickup and her eyes stared into mine. 'We just can't rehome her. That's not what we're about. We don't have the resources or the space. Although, we found room for Big Lad ...'

Emma had that look on her face again. 'Now that Ellie's been adopted by Valeri and Nellie, we could make space. If we hand back Monika, she's—'

'Oh, it's Monika, is it? You've named her.' I couldn't help but feel delighted. There was a reason I married this woman. Both of us knew that once Monika was back to full health, we'd have to let her come back to a life chained up in a vegetable patch. Legally, we had absolutely no choice.

With a few words to her owners promising that we would be in touch, I drove away from the vegetable garden. In the wing mirror, I saw Monika's chain discarded on the ground, not a food or water bowl in sight.

There was always hope. There have been so many uplifting moments that even when things felt as if they were going to engulf us and become too much, good things happened. Monika's owners ultimately decided that they no longer had any use for this nine-year-old dog, so they allowed her to come and live with us. We made sure that along with small amounts of regular food, she got a lot of love.

We weren't – and probably will never be – in a position to keep every dog that crosses our threshold. We don't have the room or the finances for that, yet for the coming months at least, Monika had a home.

Dawn Hillson, adopted Monika

Back in November 2016, my husband David and I waited in the kitchen at Dogs 4 Rescue in Manchester while they brought a few dogs to us, one at a time. We didn't mind what breed or type of dog we had, as long as she or he got on with our cocker spaniel, Jarvis. Straight away David took to Monika. She was such an amazing dog with the most brilliant personality. She passed away in April 2023, aged fifteen. Of course, we were devastated, yet so glad for the six and a half years she was with us.

This was the first time I heard about Street Hearts: we were told that Emma and Anthony had rescued her from a vegetable garden where she was starving to death. I've since been in touch with Emma a lot, having built up a friendship. I still have the letter that she sent me thanking us for taking Monika on board. Emma had to take the chance that if they sent her to England, someone would adopt her. In actual fact, she was only at Dogs 4 Rescue for one week before we fell for her and took her home.

Many rescue dogs who aren't used to being in a home are wary, especially of men. Monika was so nervous when she first arrived. A sudden noise, like a cork popping, frightened her. Possibly this reaction from her was because the vegetable garden where she'd been chained up was in close proximity to hunters' cabins. The noise might have been something she associated with the sound of gunshots. Traffic used to scare her too. She had spent years away from roads, so it was something she hadn't come across before. We took her on lots of short walks, and over time, Monika built up her confidence to the point that she loved her long countryside walks. It took a couple of years for her to become the self-assured dog she later was. I remember walking her, and a cat was walking along in front of her. The cat turned back towards her and they kissed each other on the nose. That just doesn't happen; it was lovely.

Monika didn't like another dog to be behind her. I suppose it was years of being chained up with no way of fending off the male dogs who repeatedly mated with her. If Jarvis walked behind her, she would snap at him. Then, after a few months, it suddenly didn't bother her at all and she stopped snapping at him.

We hadn't had her long when a French stick went missing from the kitchen worktop. Monika had snuck away with it, ripped it in two, placed one piece halfway up the stairs and the other partway towards the loft. With nowhere to dig and bury her find, she was trying her utmost to hide food. All those years of being starved were still with her. It was a month after she got here that she decided that her sleeping spot was no longer on her bed outside our bedroom door. Monika barged past David and came into our bedroom. That was now her spot.

Jarvis taught Monika how to be excited. Despite his senior years, he could act crazy and would stretch his front legs in front of him and rest on his elbows in a play bow. Monika looked at him, saw what he did and copied him so that she could show her excitement too.

The entire family had so much bereavement and upset just over a year after Monika came into our lives. Firstly, we moved house, then our son Declan passed away in November 2017, and then the following month, Jarvis died. Everything happened in such quick succession, yet Monika was adept at adapting to such sad losses and change.

I didn't go into work for a time after our son's death, so my mum looked after Monika. My mum isn't a dog person but told me that she would happily have kept her. That's how much of an amazing dog she was – she won people over. She was always good with people, cats and other dogs.

When we were in the right position to open our family home to other dogs, we adopted two further rescues: Henry from Yorkshire and Gary from Cyprus. Monika, who was by now the size of a portly labrador, was certainly the matriarch and was treated like the Queen.

Henry has always been the most problematic out of the three of them, while Monika was the calming influence. I think that's why the other adoptees worked out so well. She had such a unique personality and was an older dog too. I think that older rescue dogs also have an appreciation of their newfound situation that other dogs don't have. I would never buy a dog again, only ever adopt.

David tells me that his best memory of Monika was simply, everything. He doesn't think there will ever be another dog as good as Monika, it was every single thing about her that made her special.

Anyone adopting a rescue should expect things to take time. Don't expect change too quickly, as the dog needs time to adjust. Slowly build up to situations and you'll be rewarded in exchange. Enjoy your dog's development.

11.

Roshy the Wonder Dog

Emma – Then – May 2016

Anthony and I were fixated by this point: our every waking thought – plus a few in our dreams – came back to how we could help every street dog. We had as many of them neutered as possible and tried to make sure that the sick and injured ones had the veterinary care they needed. Even so, we had both dismissed the idea of a shelter. Not only was it a far cry from anything we'd intended, but we didn't know how we would get it off the ground. Even with Tipsy, Little Blackie, Big Lad, Ellie and Monika, we were absolutely not going to open and run a shelter.

Then along came Roshy.

We were told that a large street dog was living about forty-five minutes' drive from our house, and he had made his home by a petrol station. I set out to find him and to see what we could do for him. The first visit ended without me catching him, as did the second and the third, and ... well, you get the picture. I saw this massive long-haired mess of a dog and he got away from me every time. He was having none of it. I had several round trips of an hour and a half, but I was determined not to give up. A couple of times I managed to creep towards him with some food and get a good look. He was in horrific condition, with such terrible mange that his skin looked like elephant hide. It took me ages to capture him, the allure of dog food wasn't the pulling power I had hoped it would be. Eventually Anthony came with me, and, with no other choice, we darted him with the tranquiliser gun. Even then he managed to give us the run around. I was falling in love with this dog and his antics.

People from the factory nearby came out and started to shout at us that they loved him too and we couldn't take him. I asked them which one of them was going to take the dog to the vet and get him treated but oddly no one volunteered.

Roshy was probably the first dog we had caught with serious mange, and he had an old injury to his back hips, so he was a bit of a cronky old thing. At that point our land wasn't properly fenced, and we didn't have proper pens, drainage or water stations, so it was basically our home, complete with a couple of dozen dogs we had taken in.

Roshy's skin was so bad he developed a massive abscess, and we were draining two litres of fluid off him a day. It was clear he would have died quite quickly if we hadn't intervened. It was the last time we used the dart gun, although I don't know how we'd have caught him without it.

We spent ages trying to make friends with Roshy. We bathed him so many times. We don't use the same skin treatments now, but at the time, a lot of it was trial and error because of the awful state he was in. I learnt a lot about skin problems because of this one particular street dog. We deal with mange differently today too. At the time, we needed to treat the mange and get the lice out from under his skin. Another problem we had to overcome was the chronic ear infections that Roshy always suffered from. Mange gets into dogs' ears and his had very thick cartilage, which easily became encrusted.

Once he got his paws under the table, Roshy had a great trick of taking the scared dogs away from the shelter off into the forest and failing to bring them home at night. I suppose he was trying to get his own back for all the bathing, tick-removing and mange treatments. He spent most of his life laughing at me trying to get hold of him. His defiance made me love him that little bit more. Eventually he came and lived in the house with us, cuddling up in his bed at night. He was a legend, an absolute legend.

Roshy always stank and did so until the end of his days. But while he might have been pungent, he was a prime example of how extraordinary dogs can be. Roshy gave us so much back: he taught me how to deal with really scared dogs and that dogs can heal other dogs. As more and more dogs crossed our threshold, Roshy would bring even the very scared ones to me. Over time, I got to know them all and helped them understand that they were being taken care of. He then did it again and again with quite a few of the dogs in and around our home. He also took the scared dogs away from me when he thought they had had enough. He was intuitive and didn't only help other dogs, he helped me. I can't describe the connection I had with him. I could look into his soul and, I think, vice versa. I spent a lot of time brushing that great big bear of a dog, and, of course, just loving him. He was so stubborn and that's why I loved him so much.

It was because of this extraordinary dog that Anthony and I had the conversation about whether we really should and could become a shelter. We knew that we couldn't put Roshy back on the streets, so he was here to stay. He took us one step closer to realising that if we actually did open our home to as many dogs as possible, we could help so many more lost souls like him.

Anthony and I understood that the only way to cope with the sheer volume of dogs that we were bringing in was to rehome some of them. There was no legal licensing requirement for us to do so at this time, but it was on the horizon and when the time came, we would have to be ready. In the meantime, we had to start finding adopters for some of the dogs we had. Not Roshy, not Tipsy, not Big Lad and the others that were, and always will be, our dogs, but the others that were coming to us thick and fast. Our social media pages started to gain momentum; people were showing an interest in adopting the dogs that were ready to find what we began to call their 'furever homes'.

We only considered a dog to be ready once it was neutered, vaccinated, in full health and we knew that we weren't setting up dog and adopter for a fall. The only way we could get the dogs to their destination was through a third-party transportation company in Bulgaria. But we soon came to realise we would have to take on the transport trips ourselves. We worked with another charity to rehome the dogs once they were in the UK. Things sometimes didn't work out for the dog, and it was only afterwards that we heard that one or two of the dogs were being abandoned back into UK rescue centres. While overseas rescue dogs equate to a tiny proportion of the dogs in UK rescue centres, one is too many.

Armed with the knowledge that we would need to become a licensed shelter, and do it fast, we needed to operate our own safe delivery of the dogs and take control of every aspect of the process. These dogs had endured too much, come too far, to end up in a worse situation. We needed a new plan. But we were a team. We could do this.

12.

Foreign Dogs

Anthony – Now

One of the first things that visitors to our Street Hearts BG website see is the number of dogs we've had neutered. At the time of writing, it stands at over 4,000. Emma and I have overseen the rehoming of 1,402 dogs from the streets of Bulgaria to British, German, Belgian and Austrian adopters. These are figures we're extremely proud of, but our biggest aim is to put ourselves out of business. Not only would it make our lives much more sedate, but more importantly it would mean that dogs aren't suffering neglect, cruelty and starvation.

Simply put, the dogs we rescue and – with the help of hundreds of amazing adopters – rehome should never have been born in the first place. They are animals that have been dumped once they're no longer needed or wanted, or thrown away like rubbish when they become a nuisance.

Today's transportation from Dryanovo to England starts for me and Lauren Hoodless, our shelter manager, as soon as the dogs are ready. Once they've been walked, videoed for their eagerly awaiting new families and loaded onto the bus, we are on the road. It's normally a surprisingly easy task to get all twenty dogs inside their crates in the back of the bus. The trips are exhausting but it's the heart of why we do this. Pre-Brexit, we were moving twenty dogs to the UK every three weeks. Now it's twenty dogs every five weeks, yet still it takes a lot of stamina to do these trips.

We've fitted out two buses – Frankie the Furever Bus and Renée the Rescue Bus – specially for this purpose, ensuring they could be licensed by the Bulgarian authorities and comply with European standards. It took around fourteen days to fully convert each one with a fitted deck to carry a second layer of cages – to comply with Bulgarian and European law, they can only be two levels high – with each cage mechanically fixed to the structure. The buses must be temperature-controlled and include bunk beds for two people.

As we always turn everything into a positive, I had made good use of travel restrictions due to an African swine fever outbreak by spending time at home readying Frankie for its inaugural trip in August 2019. The outbreak stopped all EU animal transport travelling through Hungary, and as we fall under general animal transport laws and have to pass through Hungary to get to the UK, the dogs – and me – had to stay in Bulgaria. Eventually they excluded dogs from what was really a ban on the movement of livestock, so that we could travel again. The only real effect for us was that we had far too many dogs: up to 140 at one point. It was absolutely hideous. The dogs couldn't go anywhere, but there were still a lot on the streets that needed our help, so they kept coming. It made everything extremely busy and stressful, with dogs absolutely everywhere.

Before we had Frankie and Renée we had used a bus I had bought while still working offshore as a commercial diver that we'd named Frieda the Furever Bus, and when I crashed it in May 2019, I was devastated. How do you get dogs 2,000 miles across a continent without a suitable vehicle? I thought it was the beginning of the end. The money was running out as the shelter grew and grew; more dogs meant more vet's bills, more food, more pens and more adoptions and rehoming.

Most of the business-minded people we knew suggested a fundraiser, but we were so reluctant. What would people think? Our everyday personal and work business is done in a Toyota pickup we bought long before Street Hearts existed, but would people know and appreciate that? How important would people on the outside think a new bus was? Of course, the new bus wasn't for us, it was for taking the adopted dogs to their new homes. Regardless, we knew there would be backlash.

Emma and I pondered it for quite a while, but in the end we decided that we had no choice but to give it a go. Within twenty-four hours of the appeal going live, we'd raised more than half of the money. The support that we had was incredible, immense, and way beyond our expectations. Of course, there were the naysayers who said that we were only interested in getting a fancy vehicle, but these weren't the people who were driving 4,000 miles across Europe with twenty dogs on board for the outward leg. We couldn't afford breakdowns, we couldn't afford to miss the Channel Tunnel crossings, and we couldn't afford delays in the documents we needed. But the 440+ people who donated seemed to get it.

Our hearts sank when the state vet informed us that we needed a second vehicle in case of emergency backup for a breakdown or accident. We have international insurance, but no one is coming out to rescue twenty dogs from the back of a bus. The second bus was needed so that someone could drive out and get the dogs if things went wrong.

Emma and I had the same dilemma over the fundraiser for the second bus. We couldn't just rent one as it would have to be fitted out to a certain standard, licensed and available immediately. We understand that people are rightly cautious. But fortunately we have a legion of supporters who have done so much to help these dogs in a faraway country that most of them have never set foot in. Emma and I wouldn't be able to do a fraction of what we do for the dogs if it wasn't for the endless support we get.

This morning, as the dogs bound around us, aware something is about to happen, the rest of our ever-expanding Street Hearts team is on hand to say a tearful farewell. Emma and Lucy, our full-time Bulgarian outreach worker, have readied and cleaned the crates for our departees, added a non-slip bowl of water for each dog and made sure the mountain of paperwork is all in order. As we start to crate train all the dogs long before we set off, it's usually excitement that holds us up rather than any kind of apprehension. Other than the odd whine for attention, the only sound coming from the back of the canine-filled van, as I take a look inside, is a soft thudding from a dozen or so tails tapping against the metal sides of their crates. After a last run-through of the inventory – dogs, food, water, paperwork, human carry-on – Emma and the others say their final farewells to the dogs – and we're ready.

Our first quick stop before we're finally on our way is to see Julian Petkov, who owns the local petrol station. As well as checking our tyres, Julian still keeps a close eye out for any stray dogs. Over time, he has found something like fifty or sixty street dogs here that people have abandoned or dumped, probably travelling distances to do so. It used to be every week or so that he would call us out, but things have slowed down these days. Once he has declared the tyres fit for the journey, we're off across Europe. We drive for four and a half to five hours until, about thirty minutes shy of the Danube and close to the Bulgaria–Romania border, we make our first scheduled break. The border is a hard stop, meaning we may be detained and inspected, leading to delays. We don't feed the dogs before we set off, so this is also an opportunity to top up their water bowls, give them some food and walk them. Lauren and I take two dogs each at a time, return to the van and change them over so everyone gets a leg stretch and a chance to relieve themselves.

It's also another perfect moment in the trip for us to send the excited adopters in the UK some videos and photos of their dogs. Laura Norrey, our adoption co-ordinator, takes care of administration and adoption processes; fosters dogs in England for us on occasion; and co-ordinates the entire operation, running it from her home. She will have set up a WhatsApp group for each transportation run with all those receiving dogs included. They can also track our live location as we cross the continent. Think of it as the Santa Express for dog adopters.

Emma takes care of the paperwork well in advance of us setting off and makes sure that, along with all the legal requirements, the new owners are aware of any medical needs of their new pets. Every single one of our dogs is fully vaccinated, neutered, microchipped, wormed, given flea treatment and blood tests taken for parasites and diseases before they are allowed to travel. Plus, of course, they have a Pet Passport.

Before our vet Dimitar neuters the dogs, he takes a blood sample at his practice. Part of his training was studying exotic diseases, and we've recently upgraded the tests to polymerase chain reaction (PCR) testing. The diseases these kits test for are all caused by parasites, such as ticks, mosquitos, sand flies. Sand flies are something that comes from Mediterranean countries, but recently they have been found in remote parts of Bulgaria, nowhere near sand or water. The blood tests he uses include testing for leishmaniasis, which is a protozoan parasite and is not curable.

The other blood tests also screen for brucellosis, heart worm and tick-borne diseases. Brucellosis is quite a hot topic in the UK at the moment and some UK vets insist on a second test when a Street Hearts dog gets adopted. Our advice is to change vets – we've already made sure the tests are carried out. With Dimitar's help, we make sure that the dogs are fit and healthy before they travel. Many diseases can stay in the blood and remain dormant, so testing is important. All of the blood tests are run at the same time and it's perfectly routine that the dogs test positive for one type of tick or another. If so, they are treated with antibiotics prior to transport. Our aim is that we have the dogs tested well above the minimum requirements.

Lauren and I take it in turns to take and share photos, quickly followed by a raft of heart and thumbs-up emojis from the rest of the group. We've seen this escalating excitement many times, and it's a joy to be a part of something so positive. Lauren is also on hand to answer any questions or queries that might crop up. Adopters' questions increase, the closer we get to them.

Sadly, the comments we get on social media aren't always as positive. Some people think we should leave the dogs where they are; that we have enough stray dogs of our own in the UK. I suspect these same people have pure-bred dogs costing thousands of pounds, keeping the breeders in financial clover. The breeding conditions often mean that there is either something genetically wrong with the dogs or they are simply surplus to requirements. Rescue centres in the UK are generally full of breed dogs, all bought and surrendered for whatever reasons. They are usually UK bred and not foreign dogs which make up a very small percentage.

We're not adding to the problem at Street Hearts; we're trying to reduce it. The dogs we rehome should never have been born. With the neutering and education programme we run, we are stopping overseas dogs from being taken to the UK in the first place. So many people who adopt from us tell us that they've tried to rescue a dog in the UK but faced so many restrictions around their working hours, the size of their garden and ages of their children, it has made it impossible for them to adopt from a local or national charity. Others have told me about dogs they've adopted without having been warned of behavioural issues that quickly manifest themselves. We purposely don't send aggressive dogs to adopters, even if 95 per cent of the time, the dog is perfectly well behaved. Dogs like Big Lad will always stay with us and live out their days at Street Hearts. All dogs on our website have a short biography stating whether they should be an only dog, if they're good with older children or whether they've been 'cat tested'. That way, people are armed with all of the facts, and we get few failed adoptions.

The same people who make these comments possibly avoid spending time on the rest of our social media feed. We post footage from villages in Dryanovo and Tryavna, where we've been alerted to dogs in dire need of rescuing. To help highlight what goes on here, we record and show the awful conditions some of our rescues have lived in, sometimes for years, with no proper food, shelter, or fresh water. These soul-wrenching scenes don't usually attract 'leave them where they are' comments. Seeing a dog trapped behind a wire fence, fastened to a rickety lean-to by a three-foot long chain, nothing but mud to stand in and rotting bread to eat, doesn't tend to elicit the same responses as the photos of happy, playful, well-fed dogs off to new homes with caring families.

I've never regretted the decision to move to Bulgaria. The initial thought behind it might have been partly due to the cost of living and house prices, but I had already seen for myself how great this country can be. The street dogs were something we just couldn't ignore. Everything we've done has brought us to where we are now. There might have been things that we could have done differently. It's evolved and it's evolving. We find that we're doing things and we're doing them well and then something will happen and we think, hang on, we should have been doing it like that all along and so we adapt. That's almost daily, especially the way that we interact with dogs and how we train them. We deal with staff issues; it's constantly changing and evolving. We look over things that haven't quite gone to plan and take them as lessons learnt; with the promise to do better next time. We can only move forward, and that's what we're doing, moving forward.

Each time I make the journey to the UK, it's either with Lauren or Lucy. Emma usually stays at Street Hearts to take care of absolutely everything else while we're gone. Lauren has been a permanent team member at our shelter since the end of 2021. She knows the dogs and the journey by now. The trips are always spent chatting about our latest rescues and updating the current adopters, interspersed with eating a lot of chocolate. I drive while Lauren uploads the newest photos, until we stop again and swap over. Every stop we make is a chance for the dogs to get out and for us to clean their crates and refill their bowls.

I'm never sure how long the border crossing to Romania will take. It's a non-Schengen border so it's a hard stop. Although Frankie and its cargo is less than 3.5 tonnes, meaning we can avoid joining the lorry queue of up to 30 km long, it can still take anywhere from twenty minutes to three hours for our bus to make it across. Today, luck is on our side and it's only half an hour.

We have four days of driving, as many nights of sleeping on board and something like fifteen hours of dog walking before we reach our final destination. Some of the dogs we're taking to their new lives came to us as puppies, and so their existence as street dogs was mercifully short. Others were not so fortunate.

From when we started our shelter in 2016, we've seen some change for the better in attitudes towards dogs in Bulgaria. Even so, there are moments that stick in my mind and dogs that won't ever leave my thoughts. It's these moments that make the 4,000-mile, eight-day round trip, sleeping in a bus, ten-fold-increased-post-Brexit paperwork all worthwhile.

13.

Garden of Doom

Emma – Then – September 2016

I shouted to Anthony that I was about to head out to Gesha village. I had already told him that a woman in Dryanovo town had let me know about a garden where a number of dogs were living. From her description, I wasn't entirely sure that living was the right word. Anyway, I got into the pickup with a container of water, food, bowls and the rest of my kit, and set out on a thirty-minute drive.

The day was already very warm, and even though I've always been a fan of the heat, it didn't stop me from worrying about the animals, particularly the dogs. I could only hope that a neighbour had been taking care of them in some way.

As I drove through the village, four dogs ran across the streets. There was no sign that anyone owned them, particularly as most Bulgarians keep their dogs chained up. I was certainly in the right place, so I parked and made my way to the village square, my dog-capture kit with me.

Within a couple of minutes, I was joined by an English woman who introduced herself as Jane Duberley. She had moved here from Lincoln ten years ago after retiring from her job as a betting shop manager, and she forewarned me about the dogs. It was a pitiful tale: one of her neighbours, an elderly man, had started to collect dogs in his garden. He seemingly had a fondness for them and was, in his way, helping them. Unfortunately, he passed away and the seventeen dogs on his property were left to fend for themselves.

We made our way to a house at the back of Jane's own house. Her rear garden was a short distance from a track, six-foot-high stone walls on either side. The track was wide enough for me to drive the pickup the couple of hundred metres until I reached my destination. Towards the end of the track on the right-hand side, instead of the neat stone walls indicating the boundaries of other gardens, was a tangle of thickets. It was impassable without being torn to shreds on the mess of branches, brambles and thorns. I saw the crumbling house in the distance, an old, abandoned car and what were clearly dogs. Some were moving, some were not. The only way to get to them was through a set of high metal gates to the side of the hostile hedges. The gates were corrugated metal and fortunately, not locked, merely stuck fast where the garden had tried to claim them. We forced our way in, focused on getting to the dogs. I wasn't really prepared for the devastation that greeted me.

The rest of the garden wasn't much better and the view of the dilapidated house didn't improve as we got nearer. The edifice was the least of our worries. I counted seventeen dogs in the garden. Some of the dogs were starving, their ribs protruding through their patchy, unkempt fur and some had visible tumours. All of them were covered in ticks. The ones that weren't chained up were taking shelter from the falling masonry where parts of the house were crumbling around them. As I'd suspected, there was no water for them to drink, so we could only guess when they last had any water in this unbearable heat. A couple of the dogs were in such a bad way, I knew that we were going to have to call a vet and have them put to sleep straight away. Their suffering was too much to watch.

One dog, who we decided to call Sandy, had clearly taken to living on the backseat of an abandoned red hatchback. The sight was so bizarre: the gates didn't open without a struggle, the entire garden was impenetrable shrubs, weeds and trees, and in the middle of it was a car with a dog who had made its home on the backseat.

Another of the dogs was a pregnant bitch, nothing more than a walking skeleton. We named her Rosie. It was a truly awful decision to make, but we knew that if she delivered those puppies she wouldn't survive. If she had been spayed, this situation wouldn't have happened in the first place. Despite this, we could tell from their ear tags that some of the dogs had been neutered. Whenever a vet neuters a street dog, the ears are tagged. It's similar when street cats are neutered, although a tiny part of their ear is removed to mark that it's been done. In this case, I was convinced that the guy who had owned the house was supported by another organisation who had neutered them. I could only guess that no one had informed them that the house owner had passed away.

We saw bags of food and kibble dropped into bowls and on the ground. Again, it was possibly another rescue charity that had done this. It would be easy to point the finger at someone dropping food and then walking away, but we knew how hard it was to take on dogs, any number of dogs, especially seventeen of them. Imagine finding such a scene in the UK. Now, imagine, there are no shelters, no charities with the capacity to take them; no RSPCA, no Dogs Trust and no Battersea Dogs and Cats Home. Could you take them all home?

Anthony and I were only months into establishing our shelter and in all honesty, we were skint. Regardless, Jane and I started to feed the dogs. I called Anthony and formulated a plan that over the coming weeks, we would start to pick out the remaining dogs. We talked through having the rest neutered, and with little else in place, legally or practically, we knew that rehoming them was going to take some time.

Jane and I worked our way around the Garden of Doom, giving the dogs food and water and checking them for injuries so the vet could prioritise as soon as he arrived. I knew that Anthony and I would have to settle the vet bill – it had become something of a standard procedure, but as I watched Jane out of the corner of my eye, I could see from her body language that she was finding this even harder going than I was.

'You OK?' I called over to her at one point, not entirely sure whether she was brushing away tears.

'I can't leave them like this,' she said, jamming her sunglasses back on before she looked in my direction. 'I can take one, no, two. Yes, I'll take two of them home with me.'

I straightened up to allow the circulation to flow back into my legs from where I'd been trying to comfort Rosie. She should have been the size of a labrador but I could count her ribs as she stood in front of me. Her brown and white body stayed perfectly still while I stroked the top of her head where the white stripe ran from her nose to the back of her neck. The only sign I got that she was loving the attention was her wagging tail.

'It really would be wonderful if you could,' I said. It would have been too much to hope that Jane would take Rosie; besides, she was in such a state, it was clear that she needed immediate veterinary care. 'Any help to get any of these dogs away from here would be amazing.'

Jane glanced around. Even with the dark glasses shielding her eyes, I could tell she was bewildered, not knowing where to start. I'd found a kindred spirit: her compassion was palpable.

'That one,' said Jane, pointing at a medium-sized black dog, his face as forlorn as the other sixteen. 'And that one.'

Now she appeared to be a little overwhelmed, and that was the last thing I wanted.

'OK, one thing at a time,' I told her. 'Let's wait until the vet arrives and take it from there.'

By the time the vet got to us, Jane and I had decided that I would also take two dogs with me, she would regularly feed and water the rest and that way, we could return over the coming months and do all that we could to rescue the remaining thirteen.

I pushed away the rising panic at how Anthony and I were going to cope with the twenty-two dogs we were already caring for, not to mention these two newest additions to the Smith household. Things were really starting to get out of hand.

14.

Kate: Actor, Adventurer, Dog Whisperer

Anthony – Then – Winter 2016

Things were going from strength to strength with the neutering programme. Emma and I were doing everything that we could think of to get to the stage where we were a fully licensed shelter and able to take in more and more dogs. Despite the inroads we had made, dogs were still roaming the streets, mating and breeding and finding themselves dumped indiscriminately whenever owners tired of them or they became ill. Not for the first time, we had the conversation about how we were going to pay for everything. When we'd moved to Dryanovo, we had enough money to live on, but we hadn't factored in some twenty-five dogs, and the number was going up weekly.

We knew that there was no way we could continue, yet we knew that we couldn't simply draw a line under the whole thing and walk away. We were so close to becoming a licensed shelter. As it started to look as if we were going to end up overwhelmed and unable to carry on, things took another unexpected, happy turn of events. Our social media pages meant that we were getting some inquiries from people looking to adopt the dogs that were mentally and physically ready for rehoming. At this time, adoptions from Bulgaria to other countries was quite different. The dogs didn't necessarily need to be in a licensed shelter for thirty days prior to adoption – it wasn't a requirement. Some of those who did adopt came straight to us and took the dogs back with them to Austria, Germany, even New Zealand. The rest were adopted and taken by a third-party transportation company based in Bulgaria. Out of the blue, we received an inquiry from someone called Kate Lamb who was looking to adopt a dog. I told Emma whose reaction was, 'Fine, she can apply like everyone else. Get her to fill out an application or go to a rescue centre in the UK.'

I stopped short and said, 'You do know who she is, don't you? Kate Lamb, the actress? Off the telly? *Call the Midwife* Kate Lamb?' Thankfully, Kate didn't hold Emma's initial off-hand reply against us and made the eighteen-hour journey from a snowboarding trip in Austria to spend time with us in Bulgaria.

For so long it had been just Emma and me, with sporadic visits from family and friends to give us a hand. Kate was a completely different entity. As well as her career as an actress, her adventurer attitude and animal-loving personality, she was a whirl of energy. We instantly loved her enthusiasm and commitment. Along with her many other talents, Kate is a dog behaviourist and offers her services to dog owners in London and the Home Counties. While she was here with us, she coached Emma and me in lead training the dogs and quietly demonstrated her skills.

Amongst her various interests and endeavours, Kate also takes part in parkour and bouldering in the United Kingdom and throughout Europe. This was the unlikely connection that led her to us. Bulgaria has some excellent bouldering areas, and, even though we didn't know the connection at the time, friends of hers from the London parkour and climbing community had rented our bungalow. With funds drying up, it had dawned on us that we needed income for our rapidly growing dog food bills, so renting out the bungalow was a handy source of money. Kate's friends posted photos of puppies and pack walks online and it was these images that piqued her interest of this Bulgarian puppy paradise. Sadly, Kate's thirteen-year-old dog Willow had died at the end of 2016, so for the first time in years she was dogless and free to travel across Europe.

On Kate's first morning with us we caught a dog called Susie and her two six-month-old daughters who had never been handled by people before. One of the puppies took a bite out of everyone except for Kate. She started work with them immediately, using techniques and methods we didn't know about, and within six days they were lead-trained and on their way to being pets. Luna and Themba now have happy homes in the UK. Kate was also really good at catching dogs with us, crawling under cars, squeezing into gaps, all the things that we were doing on a daily basis. It was really fantastic: we'd never had this amount of dedicated help before.

One of the many dogs Kate met during her time here was Big Lad. He had been with us for eighteen months or so by this time. Like most people, we thought that dogs would be better on harnesses. But it was absolutely the wrong thing for Big Lad. We didn't really understand slip leads until Kate became involved and showed us how they benefit absolutely everything. They are the most secure way to handle the dog, are quick and easy to use and are less restrictive for the dog than a harness.

During Kate's stay, we chatted amiably about all manner of things, but particularly our plans for the shelter and the modest municipality budget we had. It was Kate who coined the name Street Hearts BG but she also set up a GoFundMe page, came up with fundraising ideas, and put together an Amazon Wishlist.

When Kate came to leave, we were keen that she should become our patron and we couldn't have been happier when she agreed. She returned to the UK with a promise to return eight weeks later. If this was what Kate had done for us on her first visit, we couldn't begin to imagine what she would do next.

15.

It's Beginning to Look a Lot Like a Shelter

Emma – Then – February 2017

If it hadn't been for Miroslav Semov, our former mayor, I honestly don't think we'd have managed what we've done. His help was invaluable, but he initially wanted a municipality shelter here. As I walked towards the kitchen door, I opened it to let the fifteen dogs out, all barking their eagerness to join the ever-increasing pack in the morning's sunshine.

I've seen some of the municipality shelters and I know they are hellholes. Anthony and I suggested to Miroslav that if we built a shelter here, Dryanovo could be spared from having one. Do we regret that decision? Sometimes, when all I'd like to do is sit and relax for an hour without thirty or so dogs wanting to jump on me. Fortunately, all of my outfits look better with dog hair.

To have the shelter in our home, we had to comply with numerous regulations, such as fences of the correct height, a clinic where we could have postmortems and a visitors' area. Initially we were given a lot of help, but some things we simply didn't know and hadn't been told. We were chastised at one point for not having a rubber stamp with 'NGO' embossed on it.

Anyway, we made a start of clearing the scrubland next to our home to expand and make a dog shelter. Anthony had that determined look about him that I knew so well. He would work non-stop to put up fencing and build dog sheds to earn that licence.

This was week three of the building project and Anthony had rarely stopped. I pushed my feet back inside my boots, wrapped myself into my coat and took him a cup of coffee. Usually, he would come into the house for a break and a rest, but the days were short this time of year, so he didn't want to lose the light.

'I always knew that buying that tractor would pay off,' I said as I held out his drink, having trudged the short distance across the icy trodden path towards him.

'Really?' he said, as he cradled the mug with both hands, the steam disappearing into the cold air. I was already shoving my hands back inside my coat sleeves. The sun was shining, so despite several inches of snow, it seemed degrees warmer than it was.

'Without a doubt,' I said. 'Everyone knows that the purchase of a ... a, er, orange tractor is the best.'

'Orange?' I couldn't tell whether he was amused or annoyed. 'It's lucky I decided to marry you, you know?'

'That's right, I remember it clearly.'

Anthony gazed across the snow-topped trees that surrounded us on three sides. 'Yes, it was a beautiful evening, the sun setting in the west over Kilimanjaro. You had a glow of excitement and anticipation.'

'What a load of old rubbish,' I said, regretting not putting a hat on for this charade. 'I think you'll find it was a pub in Yorkshire, I was tired and I wanted to go home after a crap twelve-hour response shift. And I wasn't convinced that I'd managed to wash someone's mucus out of my police shirt.'

'On second thoughts, I'd had two pints of Stella, it had gone to my head and I've regretted it ever since.'

'You can get your own coffee next time,' I said, as I moved back and removed my phone from my pocket. 'I need to get some photos of you in action for our social media pages, so down that drink and get back to work.'

'Good grief, do you ever give me a break?' said Anthony. I couldn't tell whether he was smiling or not as he had his face obscured by the mug. I went with amused but wasn't really all that bothered. It wasn't as if I was sitting idle all day. I'd already cleared the paths, broken the top of the ice on the water bowls and refilled them, fed the dogs and taken them on a pack walk in the snow. Now I had to take care of the mess. At least it was easier to spot in the pristine snow.

I stepped back and waited for Anthony to continue clearing the scrub so I could take some photos. So many people had donated money to Street Hearts BG – as we were now formally called – and we knew that the donors, quite rightly, wanted to see where their money was spent. This was going to be a space for so many dog runs which would eventually have houses for multiple dogs. We knew that we would have to aim big for our plans, although no matter how many street dogs we were prepared to take on, finances aside, it was basically Anthony and me. There is only ever so much that two people can do. For the last few weeks, we had spent many evenings around our dining table trying to get a handle on resources. One that repeatedly reared its head was volunteers. We needed more help, and if we were edging closer to getting our shelter licensed, that help would probably come in the form of volunteers. We had made a decision to welcome volunteers on a more ongoing rolling basis so that we always had people coming out and lending a hand. It was the logical next step.

While Anthony manoeuvred the tractor backwards and forwards, I snapped several pictures, happy with my work. One or two of the dogs wandered over to see what I was doing, realised it was nothing particularly fascinating and moved away again. I couldn't blame them for wanting to get back inside the warmth of the house.

I looked round at the dogs. We were missing a black labrador called Cleo; she hadn't been seen since the previous evening.

I looked up, Anthony was watching me. 'You OK?'

'It's Cleo,' I said. 'I'm really worried about her now.'

Anthony looked into the trees. 'I didn't tell you this in case she was back by now, but I heard a vehicle last night. It was driving around along the track behind the forest. Just before that, I heard a gunshot and a yelp.'

'I love that dog.' I said, 'I was going to suggest that we keep her. Roshy would be beside himself if anything happened to her, especially after all she's been though.'

Cleo's story was a particularly pitiful one. The previous summer we'd been called to a local monastery. They had a puppy, put a collar on it and secured it with a chain. No one thought to loosen or change the collar as the puppy grew into an adult labrador. The collar became embedded in its neck, and eventually the dog somehow managed to get free from the chain. That was the point when someone from the monastery thought to contact us. The dog must have been in excruciating pain from the collar which was, by now, embedded about three or four centimetres into her neck. As it was summer and extremely hot, flies were everywhere, including in the wound.

As soon as we got anywhere near her, we could smell the wound. It was disgusting. Her flesh was rotting and she was scared stiff. She continually bolted from us whenever we got close. Anthony and I were fairly new to the whole dog-capturing set-up, so our equipment was a bit on the limited side, and it took us a couple of hours to get her under control.

We took her straight to the vet, expecting that she would have to be put to sleep because of the seriousness of her injuries. Instead, Dimitar told us about a remarkable green solution called Granulin which speeds up the recovery process for wounds. He sedated her and cut the collar off. It was her entire neck; not one centimetre was spared. It was impossible to stitch the whole thing, especially as it was so deep. It was drastic, but the Granulin helped so much.

Once we got her back to the shelter, I worked with Cleo for such a long time, sitting with her for weeks and weeks. Eventually she turned a corner. However, Cleo wasn't out of the woods yet: she contracted parvovirus, a disease that is highly contagious and potentially fatal. We then had to give her multiple injections and intravenous drips, as well as other medications. That contact time during her treatment and recovery really turned her round. It happens a lot with dogs: a dog that is really wild and then becomes sick frequently learns to trust and respond more favourably to humans after being cared for so intensely. The time spent with them really helps them to become confident.

I grew to love Cleo, almost as much as Roshy, and the two dogs became inseparable, often disappearing into the forest together.

When Cleo didn't come back, we put the word out that she was missing. But it was some months before we found out what had really happened to her. One morning, Big Lad went out on the walk with the others and came running back to me with a dog's skull in his mouth. A dog's skull is very distinctive, so I knew what it was. From the shape of it, it was Cleo's. She had a particularly curved forehead that led into her nose. It could only have been her. I was so upset. She was a fabulous dog and deserved a long and happy life, not to be shot and thrown by the wayside. We never found the rest of her body.

Some days it would have been so easy to give up and go home to Britain, and this felt like one of them. That was until I caught something out of the corner of my eye. I turned and there, through the bushes, I saw a flash of light as the sun penetrated a gap in the leaves and reflected against the barrel of a gun. A man of about sixty was crouching down, watching me, and in his hands, he gripped a hunting rifle. I have always absolutely refused to be intimidated by bullies and criminals, never more so than when I'm doing the right thing.

We weren't going anywhere.

16.

Cycling Through Heatwave Lucifer

Emma – Then – August 2017

Still full of ideas, Kate Lamb had suggested that she come over, adopt a dog, and then cycle home to the UK and raise money for us. So, on 3 August 2017, I set off on my mountain bike riding beside Kate, whose newly adopted former street dog Scout was perched on the back of her bike. Somehow, I'd agreed to go with her as far as Hungary. I couldn't get cover for the whole duration of the trip, and I was secretly pleased about that when we set off in Heatwave Lucifer.

I genuinely thought I was going to die.

Kate and I set off, cycling uphill to Dryanovo to be officially seen on our way by the mayor. Other cyclists were there to wish us well and they made it quite the send-off. It was a wonderful gesture, almost as touching as the next one, 3 km further on at the next ceremony. We didn't actually get on the road until 11 a.m., and by then it was roasting. I envied Scout in her covered carrier.

The first night, we stayed with a friend of mine and then what followed can only be described as the hilliest day of my life. We travelled towards the ferry port, a rest in sight. I gave it my all, cycled to the top of an enormous hill, and felt a rush of exhilaration as I freewheeled down the other side. I stopped at the bottom to catch my breath, admiring the scenery and congratulating myself on a job well done. I waited for Kate. Then I waited some more. And I waited.

My concern mounting for Kate and Scout and, my legs screaming at me, I cycled back to the top of the hill to find them. I could make out her abandoned bike in the distance, lying on its side next to the road, the sun glinting off the frame. No sign of Kate and no sign of Scout. My heart was hammering – for more than one reason – as I frantically pushed on to her discarded bike.

I looked towards the trees that were set back from the road, momentarily unsure whether I should try to look for her or stay where I was. I saw a movement and Kate came striding through the trees, Scout beside her. 'Thanks for waiting,' she said. 'I'd dropped my GoPro, so I had to go back for it.'

I was so relieved to see her, I couldn't even be cross that I'd cycled 2 km uphill and back down again – twice!

We carried on our journey along the Transfagarasan highway, a paved mountain road through the Romanian Carpathian Mountains, admiring the scenery. In spite of the heat and hard work, I really enjoyed the journey. And when it came to say goodbye I was sad I couldn't carry on with her.

Kate raised a whopping £10,000 from the bike ride, which paid for us to have a much-needed clinic on site, boundary fencing, and some new pens so we could house more street dogs. This, plus the additional generosity of our supporters, meant that we survived. We couldn't have done it without them.

Kate also advised us on putting together a website. It was a gamble for us, as the cost to get it up and running was £500. But we made that back in one week through people's generous donations. We use social media a lot now, but at the time, it was essential that the public could see what we were doing, and we were able to share our news and updates. The geography of where we are still means that local folk don't pay us enough visits. Not everyone drives or has a car, and the steep kilometre-long track from the main road is likely to put even the reasonably curious off visiting. The website allows people to see what we do and where their money goes.

The pace of volunteers coming out here really took off around the time that Kate and I did the bike ride. The set-up for our volunteers is a far cry from what it was when we initially started to take them on. We recognised that we needed help, and dog-loving people were willing to give it. At first we had no interview process and we weren't always giving the volunteers coherent instructions or a real structure to their time here. We were keen to open the doors and show people what we could do, but perhaps our keenness was getting in the way of guidance. I also found it tricky to manage what people should be doing when we weren't even paying them. Frequently they were left to their own devices, the result being that there was no real benefit to them or us. We put them up in our house and fed them, but we knew we had to get to grips with the volunteering arrangements to make sure that everyone got the most out of it. We've come a long way and now we clearly set our expectations and think about what the volunteers will get in return.

For the first time, we had enough financial security to not only build enclosures and runs for the dogs but also to maintain them and improve the area around the farmhouse. The pathways were still mud, which made for an interesting walk in the rain. In fact, it wasn't too easy to get around in the snow and ice either. Still, Anthony had put in the foundations for the runs, erected fencing and was making full use of the orange tractor – see, I know my stuff. One day, we would be in a position to have people directly adopt from us, interviewed and screened by us, and we would be able to drive them across Europe to excited families in the UK. That was our dream.

17.

Only 1,700 Miles to Go

Anthony – Now

It's always an intense time before we set off across Europe with our precious cargo of twenty dogs. One of the many pre-departure requirements is that the state vet must come out and scan each dog. Our state vet is Dr Vasil Petrov and he has been alongside us since we became a licensed shelter. He completes so much of the documentation with us, as well as carrying out the legally required inspections. Whenever we have a legal issue it is always Vasil who helps us. He's been a lifeline for Street Hearts. He facilitates so much for us and helps with the issuing of our licences via the Food Standards Agency. It's an organisation a bit like DEFRA, but here is called BABH. His input makes the entire process a lot less stressful for humans and dogs alike.

The system specifies that dogs in a registered shelter like ours – non-legal ones clearly don't do this – are scanned and declared fit and well to travel. Their microchips are scanned – all dogs in Bulgaria should be microchipped by law – the information is downloaded, and the system churns out the documents to allow the dogs to transit through the EU, plus the certificates for importing them to the UK. We have to present BABH with a journey run and we can also download it when we're back in Bulgaria if necessary. If, for example, there has been a rabies outbreak somewhere we might have travelled through, the authorities in Bulgaria will ask us where we've been and want proof of our route. It serves a more positive purpose too. It allows adopters in the UK to track us, like Father Christmas's sleigh. If Brits are adopting a dog and it's coming from overseas, they should be able to follow the vehicle no matter which shelter they use.

Today's journey is going well: I hope I'm not too confident about the miles we're putting between Frankie the Furever Bus and Street Hearts. As we motor along, I remind Lauren of the time that we were stopped as we crossed the Romanian border, and border security wanted to inspect our cargo. That happens on occasion, but an incident I don't want to repeat involved the state vet being called out. We were delayed some time, all in the name of a random check. Once the vet arrived, it only took her fifteen minutes to satisfy herself that everything was in order, and we were on our way. As things are, we've got another three and a half days to go, and it's a delay we could do without.

It can take us about four or five hours to cross Romania. On our next scheduled stop, we go through the normal routine and get some sleep. We'll be here for around eight or nine hours, depending on how the dogs are.

We walk the dogs two at a time, Petra and Roxy excited to be the first off the bus. I fix their leads to their collars and when Lauren has hold of their leads, she clips a second one for each dog to her safety belt. We take no chances! Prior to their European road trip, the dogs have been walked around Dryanovo town centre several times to familiarise them with traffic and crowds. However, nothing is quite the same as a motorway truck stop.

Lauren and I are used to the long journey now and know that we'll get a reasonable night's sleep in our bunk beds. The dogs make little noise once they've been exercised and fed. It's a chance for us to stretch our legs too and we've not even broken the back of the trip yet. It's a long distance to drive, but I'm a qualified transport manager from a former job as a lorry driver and it helps that I know what I'm doing. We adhere to all the rules, regulations and guidance when we're travelling.

Lauren takes the dogs over to the rough ground by the edge of the truck stop. Between getting food, water and clean bedding ready for Petra and Roxy, I glance at the bus. The sign writing is in English with links to our social media and the words 'Live animals in transit' in large letters. Despite everything we've done, the amount we've achieved since January 2016, I still fear that there will come a point that adopting dogs from overseas is no longer allowed in the UK. All due to unscrupulous so-called charities. The paperwork, if done correctly, is expensive and the return trip costs us around £2,500, not including the four days each way. It won't be the shelters like us that ruin it for everyone; it will be the ones who are purely making money.

Lots of people are abusing the system. If I ever park in a service station and another van transporting dogs pulls up beside me, I move our bus because I don't want to be associated with the unlicensed ones. The Bulgarian authorities clamped down on overseas dog adoptions and most of the people who were transporting dogs at that time had their licences removed and were shut down. We obtained our licence just as they were having theirs taken away. So here we are, slowly and surely making our way safely and legally across the continent.

The last ten years has thrown up challenge after challenge, with a few dilemmas along the way. Buying the house next door to us where Lucy, our other full-time team member lives, was a massive dilemma. There was no way on earth that we could have anyone else buy that house across the track metres from our front gate. It would have interfered so much with what we do. Other than the simple act of people passing up and down the lane at random times, which would have set the dogs off barking and then the neighbours complaining about the noise, the disturbance would have caused upset for our dogs. Plus, the house is supplied by water from our well, so that might have resulted in supply issues for water for us or the dogs. The absolute worst fear for us was the thought of a hunter buying it. If a hunter moved in with twenty hunting dogs barking constantly, I don't know how we would have been able to carry on. Hunters have caused us so many problems over the years, coming onto our land, driving at us, shooting at the dogs, threatening us and the dogs. The situation would have got out of hand very quickly.

Emma and I had to find the means to buy the house. We knew it wouldn't be easy to raise the money, and we knew that a small percentage of people would think that we had unscrupulous reasons for doing so. We launched the fundraiser and waited for the backlash that we were expecting people to pay for our second property. Yes, some negativity inevitably came our way, but we raised about a third of the €60,000 asking price and used our contingency fund for the rest. We'd been saving for eight years, and the money was our emergency nest egg in case we had absolutely no other way of running the shelter. It was a gamble, and it made us nervous, but not as nervous as we'd have been with hunters living metres from our gate. It gives you some idea of how desperate we were to avoid that happening. We had to put some of the money towards separating the two floors into apartments. Lucy lives upstairs and the volunteers stay in the two-bedroom apartment on the ground floor. The financial commitment to the house purchase meant that if everything went pear-shaped, we wouldn't have the money to repair the shelter. But there's no point in worrying about it – nothing is ever achieved by worrying.

While all the dogs for this particular journey across Europe have adopters eagerly waiting on their safe delivery, that wasn't always the case. Previously, when we had an older dog, like Monika who we took from the vegetable garden where she was chained and starved, we understood that she might have stood a better chance of adoption at Manchester-based charity Dogs 4 Rescue, than via Street Hearts. Monika needed to be seen for a family to realise how amazing she was. That was where Dogs 4 Rescue in Manchester came in and supported us in finding a new home and a loving family for this remarkable dog.

With every dog walked, fed and watered we can think about calling it a day – a very long day – and getting some rest ourselves.

Then we're on our way to Hungary.

18.

From Devon to Dryanovo

Emma – Then – September 2017

I was in a bit of a panic on the day that Dan Gorman arrived in our lives. Anthony and I had been out the previous day trying to catch a dog in one of the local villages. As the dog fled across a farmer's field, it made short work of leaping over a metre-high stone wall, so I followed it. My police pursuit days weren't quite behind me and I scrambled after the dog that was by then heading for the treeline. I made it to the top of the wall and jumped. Handily, what might otherwise have been a clumsy landing was broken by a plank of wood with a rusty nail sticking out of one end. The nail went straight through my foot. Anthony's 'What did you do that for?' didn't ease the pain in any way, so off we went to accident and emergency for a tetanus. On the plus side, Anthony went after the dog and caught him while I limped back to the pickup, hoping that the bleeding wasn't going to pool inside both my boot and the footwell.

The time away from the shelter I needed to recover put me behind with everything else we needed to do, especially with a brand-new volunteer arriving. Up to this point, many of the volunteers had been family and friends, but now we were formalising everything and very much learning on the job ourselves, we made sure that applications were filled out correctly and we were carrying out proper interviews.

Anthony and I had interviewed Dan who told us that he had grown up and lived in Devon, loved animals and wanted to spend his life working with them. He was coming out here for three weeks, having taken time away from his administrative job at Devon County Council. He told us that his current role was a far cry from what he actually wanted to dedicate his time to. We had considered his application carefully and thought long and hard about whether he was right for Street Hearts. In the interview, Dan came across really well and spoke about the time he had spent in South Africa, gaining amazing experience working with rhinos, cheetahs and hippos. Great skills to have if he decided to work in a zoo, but there aren't many of these creatures roaming the Bulgarian countryside. The stumbling block for us was that he didn't have any experience being around dogs, let alone working with them. But he was enthusiastic and passionate and we really warmed to him.

By now, we were at forty-five dogs. And some cats – we had cats too. Perhaps a zoo wasn't such a far-off idea. I had been dropping not very subtle hints to Anthony that I wanted chickens. Free-range rescue chickens would definitely fit with the non-profitable business model. I decided to work on Anthony and bide my time.

We had very recently taken in a tiny puppy that we had called Skye – another pup we found dumped in a litter bin. She was adorable, stank and was full of fleas and ticks, so one of the first tasks for Dan was going to be bath time for Skye. She was a sweet little golden puppy, possibly labrador in there somewhere, and I thought it would be a good place for him to get his hands dirty – or wet, or both. Once he arrived from the airport, I would show him to his room in the farmhouse, give him a tour and introduce him to the dogs, and then he could get stuck in.

Anthony and I both immediately liked Dan. What he lacked in experience with dogs, he made up for in devotion to helping them and getting on with it. From the moment he arrived, he was willing to take on anything and get involved in capturing street dogs, sitting with them when they needed reassurance, walking them on the pack walks and clearing up after them. There is always clearing up to do, and Dan never complained or shied away from a task.

I'd recently returned from an excellent course with the Dogs Trust in England. I took so much away from it, including learning about dog behaviour, dog school and managing the dog population humanely. I still had ideas to implement that would make our doggy park and pens as stimulating as possible. Along with the training Kate Lamb had shown us, I had changes to introduce to how we dealt with the dogs and different techniques. And, pivotal to Dan's arrival, I had learnt about structuring volunteers' time while they were here and making clear what we required from them.

Dan took all of this in his stride, moved into our home for three weeks, ate with us, laughed with us and felt our frustrations at the ongoing, and sometimes seemingly never-ending flow of street dogs.

The pack walks took place twice a day, Dan clearly loving and relishing each one. Other than the fun parts of volunteering, we gave him dog runs to clear up and water bowls and buckets to clean and fill. This required dragging a hosepipe across the yard to each kennel. Even when it rained – and at times it rained a lot – I would watch Dan slip and slide in the mud, never giving in even when his feet didn't find any purchase on the unmade paths. Anthony and I were used to it, but our volunteers weren't always prepared.

It must have been an eye-opening experience for Dan. He came out with us in the pickup to catch starving street dogs whose ribs were sticking out through their fur and whose tails were so tucked underneath them they were almost touching their stomachs while they foraged for food in the sharp spiky undergrowth. We rescued from parks and fields dogs that had been dumped by their owners when they were old and sick. Abandoning animals isn't only a Bulgarian trait: expats often buy houses here, collect dogs and other animals and then up and disappear, leaving the animals to fend for themselves. Dan, Anthony and I went out and rescued litter after litter of puppies from villages, roadsides, fields and then tried to find homes for Velvet, Gally, Snowy, Kirby and Tika. The list went on, yet nothing dampened Dan's spirits.

On Dan's last day, Anthony and I watched him navigate the mud path from the house to the dog runs, a bag of dog food in each arm and a look of determination on his face. Where the unmade paths were uneven, he slipped and fell, still clinging onto the bags. Big Lad and Tipsy rushed over to drip water and shake mud all over him as he lay prone. At least he was laughing.

'Get up,' shouted Anthony. 'What do you think this is? A holiday camp?'

Dan continued making his way to the food bins to top them up for the next day's feed. 'Same time next year, Dan?' I called out to him above the driving rain. He nodded as he tipped the dry food into the waterproof containers.

'I hope he comes back,' I said to Anthony who was a metre or so away from me.

'I've got a feeling he will,' said Anthony.

Dan Gorman, volunteer

I had the most incredible time at Street Hearts. For someone who hadn't spent much time with dogs to suddenly be surrounded by so many was quite something. The pack walks are unique and memorable to everyone who experiences them. To have dozens of dogs off the lead, walking through the fields and forests around the shelter, is quite a spectacle to behold.

Your first thoughts are 'don't the dogs run off?' and 'do they always follow you?' For the most part, they stay with you and wherever you decide to go, they follow. Once the dogs get to know you, you can take them out on the pack walks by yourself.

There were periods when it was just three of us at the shelter, so we'd often take the dogs out alone, while the other two did vet runs or cleaned the pens and put food out. You got used to the experience very quickly, as you were doing two pack walks a day and it became a normal part of your life. Every now and then, though, you'd stop and think what an incredible thing it was to be able to do this. It was always so much fun to take the dogs and explore the forest to find new routes to walk and ways to tire them all out. I remember getting lost a few times, but the dogs were generally pretty good and knew which direction to head. A pack walk at Street Hearts should definitely be on the list of 100 Things To Do Before You Die.

In the pre-fence era, whenever we came back from the evening pack walk, it would be time to put the dogs to bed. Because they weren't contained, it often took a long time to get them all to their sleeping areas. They'd go off into the trees, bushes and fields and you had a job rounding them all up. It was all part of the experience.

Emma and Anthony are such lovely people and made me feel so welcome, feeding me and allowing me into their home. They don't just help dogs, they help people as well. I left with so many happy and positive memories, thinking that I would learn Bulgarian and come back.

19.

The Rocky Road to Rufus

Anthony – Then – November 2017

Emma and I were sorry to see Dan leave and return to the West Country. He told us that he would be back, and we hoped that was true. In the meantime, we didn't have time to lament his departure. Not only were more volunteers coming, we needed to sort out the kilometre-long mud track leading to our home. While not a top priority in dog-catching terms, it's a steep incline and even the tractor sometimes had problems getting up and down it. Kate had been visiting us the previous January when it was about minus 15 degrees centigrade, and the track was icy. We had gone out to catch some puppies that were hiding under a bridge a few kilometres from Glushka and after waiting ages for them to poke their heads out, we got them and brought them to the safety of the pickup truck. On the way home, the truck couldn't make it up the track. It slid backwards on the ice and smashed into a wall, but mercifully no humans or puppies were harmed in the making of this fiasco. I walked home, got the tractor and in the process of

115

towing the pickup, the tractor slipped backwards and smashed into the front of the pickup. At least we made it home with the puppies.

No one fancied further accidents, so I set about improving the track. There were many occasions that people would arrive at the bottom of the track and dump their dogs without even bothering to walk to the house. If we can take them, we will, but frequently people won't travel that little bit further. We've found them on the field in front of our house, dumped in the bushes beside the track, and once, a neighbour at the bottom of the lane asked us to stop as we drove past. He pointed to two puppies that had been left in a tyre at the side of his shed, which is beside the lane to the shelter. They were well hidden in this tyre and there was no way we would have spotted them if he hadn't alerted us to them.

To get our shelter licence, one of the stipulations was that our lane had to be on a map, and it very much wasn't. Mayor Miroslav Semov sent a surveyor to take a look and, literally, put us on the map. While that was going on, I was adding gravel to the lane and taking care of the drains. The weather can be extreme here and almost like a microclimate. I can drive through sunshine and suddenly hit torrential rain, and when the rain comes down like a tropical storm near to our house, the water runs off the hills at an alarming rate. Over time, we watched where the water went and worked with it. We've built dozens of storm drains around our property in the exact place where the water flows, as well as digging deep channels into the forest above the house. That way the water is diverted to the storm drains before it reaches the house and dogs.

When the surveyor was here inspecting the lane, he said that once it was surveyed and on the map, it would have to become municipality property. I went ballistic. Apart from the personal cost to Emma and me, I had spent days and days building a lane for our safe passage so that we could drive around Dryanovo trying to stop their street dog problem. 'You expect me to hand it over to the municipality so that everyone can drive up here and have a picnic whenever they please?' I said. He tried to tell me that was what had to happen and I pointed out it really wasn't. I told him that I wouldn't talk to him about it again until the mayor was back from his holiday and I'd had a chance to speak to him. Ten days later, I was banging on Miroslav's door. In his authoritative way, he said to his secretary, 'Let's get this lad a coffee. I disagree with the surveyor. Why on earth would you give your property to the municipality? I wouldn't give my drive over to the municipality, I'll get the surveyor.' He called him into his office and gave him a right roasting.

While I was making no friends in the world of surveying, other things really started to gather momentum. Emma and I got a call from a couple we knew. The couple – she was Bulgarian and he was English – had been in touch with the local municipality to inform them about dogs that they had seen on the streets in Tryavna, a town about half an hour from Street Hearts. As a result of their contact, the dog catchers had descended upon the local streets and swept up any dogs they could find. After taking them to the shelter where they were neutered and ear-tagged, they took them to the couple's home and placed the three of them inside the gate to their property and left. It was standard procedure for the dog catchers to return dogs to the streets, but this was a slightly different scenario. It's important to stress that the municipality dog catchers at the time worked in a very different way to how they operate now. Sweeping up all the local street dogs they could catch and taking them to the local municipality shelter was, and still is, common practice in many parts of Bulgaria. Here, however, Emma and I got the call.

We have photographs on our social media feeds of dogs we've captured with tags in their ears prior to our vet removing them. The tags serve to show the dog's been registered and neutered at a shelter. It would be fair to say that the current shelters, while not along the same open, free-running structure that we have at Street Hearts, are an improvement on what they were when we first arrived in the country. They, like us, were overwhelmed.

With a trio of very unhappy, snarling dogs on their property, our Bulgarian–English acquaintances called Emma and me.

It was obvious to me as soon as I stepped out of our pickup that the three dogs had been drugged, most likely darted, before being dropped off. It would be impossible to neuter a dog without sedating it, but if a dog is scared and then drugged, it makes the dog even more scared.

Rufus was no exception to this: he was still only semiconscious when I arrived, but aggressive, nevertheless. He was a medium-sized dog, mostly black with tan legs, tan snout and white feet and chest. To say that he wasn't all that pleased to see me is somewhat of an understatement. The only way I had of getting him in the pickup was to throw a huge blanket over him and wrap him up to prevent him biting me. It didn't stop him from getting very mad, although it stopped me from getting ripped to pieces. It wasn't surprising he was displaying so much aggression; he was left on the street, most likely captured by use of a catchpole, drugged, ear tagged, neutered and then abandoned again.

Catchpoles – a pole with a loop at the end for hooking around the animal's neck – are widely used in Eastern Europe, but we don't favour them at Street Hearts. If a dog is under a car and it's the only way we have of getting the animal out, it's safer for everyone if we ease them out with the catchpole. It's never an option for a dog that's running away. It's an instant stop exactly like a noose around the dog's neck. It causes total fear, not to mention the injuries that can result from it. Nets are the best option, both incapacitating the dog and allowing us to administer injections without any likelihood of injury to us or the animals. At the point when I met Rufus, the number of dogs I'd captured was only in three figures. Even so, I still knew how to avoid being bitten.

Once Rufus was wrapped in the blanket, I managed to get him and the other two dogs into the pickup and drove them home. As soon as the drugs wore off and Rufus realised that he was not in any danger, he calmed down considerably.

Emma spent months working with him, sitting with him and feeding him cat food through the loop of the lead to make him comfortable with it being near him. It was months before she was able to get a lead on him, such was the negative effect of the catchpole. Occasionally we encounter a dog that doesn't get over what has happened to it, and these are frequently the ones we can't rehome. Happily, Rufus was actually a sweet, sensitive boy and one of the fortunate ones.

Once Rufus got to the stage where he was happy and confident around other dogs, he loved to roam around the shelter, going off on the pack walks. One afternoon, Rufus went out on the pack walk and didn't come back for hours. As it was getting extremely late, I went out into the yard to find him. He must have jumped the fence and collapsed outside in the summer kitchen. My relief was short-lived when I discovered what it was that had kept him out for so long. I'm still not entirely sure how Rufus managed to make it back to us before he gave in and fell to the ground. Although it was dark, I could see a massive pool of blood where he lay. I could see his lungs and internal organs. Rufus had been attacked by a wild boar and had his sides completely taken apart by its tusks. Despite his horrific injuries from an animal probably several times his size, he made it home.

Even though it was 11 p.m. on an August night, we telephoned Dimitar Dimitrov, our vet, who came straight out. Dimitar spent hours operating on Rufus, stitching him up from inside to out. The boar had torn into him, separating his lungs and diaphragm. While we awaited the outcome, Emma and I marvelled at Rufus's determination to get back to the safety of Street Hearts. There was never any doubt in our minds about what a truly remarkable dog he was, and the fact that he pulled through admirably – with a lot of help from Dimitar – says so much about him.

Once the unstoppable Rufus was back on all of his feet and ready for his furever home, we posted pictures of him on our social media feed. A good friend of ours, Karen Croft, saw him and showed some interest in him. That was enough for us; we knew what a wonderful dog he would be for the right person and we knew that person to be Karen. To be fair, we did cajole her along, possibly even as far as actively encouraging her when we knew he had caught her eye. He is the kindest, gentlest dog who deserved to catch a break.

We told Karen about the boar attack and that we hadn't been sure whether this extraordinary dog would pull through or not. We are always upfront about any medical or behavioural complications. That way, there are no surprises for adopters and no heartbreak for the dogs.

Karen went ahead and adopted Rufus. She adores him. He lives his best life on a heated floor in the kitchen, in a house with two jacuzzis – although I'm not sure he gets to use either.

20.

From Fugitive to Couch Potato

Emma – Then – June 2018

I decided to give myself a break from picking up after sixty dogs running amok in the garden, the yard and the surrounding grass and paths of our home and took a minute away from the increasing rain. A number of the dogs were taking shelter in their kennels, but the ones that weren't frolicking, had the best time splashing and rolling in the muddy puddles. I needed a few minutes in the dry.

I opened the kitchen door, some dogs using the opportunity to run outside, while others slipped back in, towards the dog beds strewn across the previously clean tiled floor.

I stepped around Little Blackie and a couple of the puppies so I could get to the sink. Out of the corner of my eye, I saw Bonnie raise her head from the sofa, her usual place of residence, shoot me a look of contempt and then fall back to sleep.

I loved Bonnie's character almost as much as Bonnie loved Roshy. Theirs was a true love story. Roshy, the great big bear of a dog who taught me so much, first brought Bonnie across the threshold into our house and helped her to overcome her fears. It amused me that she had the uncanny knack of making me feel as though I was a guest in *her* house. She would much rather we all disappeared and left her to it. She liked sleeping in a warm bed and knowing that her next meal was taken care of, but that was as much as she tolerated human interaction.

Before she joined us Bonnie had given birth to litter after litter of puppies in Dryanovo. People in town believed that Bonnie was 'their' dog, although no one wanted to take care of her offspring. And try as we might, we couldn't catch her. One morning, I was out at 5.30 a.m. trying my best to catch dogs in the pitch black. I chased one as it ran around a corner, and in the dimly lit town streets, I fell over Bonnie, who was hunkered down in a shop doorway, half of her protruding out onto the icy pavement. I made her jump out of her skin, and it didn't do me too many favours either. I thought that luck was on my side that freezing cold winter's morning by the Dryanovo Community Centre, and that Bonnie's puppy-breeding days were finally over. But, no, she got away again.

Not too long after this brief encounter with Bonnie, I started to drive across to the other side of town to feed some dogs that were living in a garden. A lovely elderly lady who used to live in the town had helped us capture and neuter these dogs, before we released them again. We didn't have the capacity to take the dogs to Street Hearts at that time, so it was the next best thing. When this lady moved away to Sofia, I drove to the garden a couple of times a week to feed them.

This particular morning, as I started to unload the food from the pickup, I heard the distinctive sound of crying puppies. It temporarily stunned me, knowing that the four dogs that were now in eager anticipation of their imminent meal had all been neutered, so none of them could have given birth under one of the many overgrown bushes or shrubs. Next to the garden was a derelict house. I stepped slowly across to the fallen-down building and followed the crying to a dilapidated shed. The roof had collapsed, the door was missing and each of the four sides was on the verge of giving in to gravity at any moment.

After four years of trying to capture Bonnie, her days on the run were up. Yes, she had given birth to another litter of puppies, but this time, I wasn't letting her get away. Despite the lack of anything like a solid structure to house her in, I managed to contain her and the puppies. I then made a hurried call to Anthony in which I failed to keep the glee out of my voice. We took her back to the shelter, had her neutered and found homes for her puppies.

There was uproar in the town that we had taken Bonnie away. We had to hide her. It felt like harbouring a fugitive, but we had little choice. The mayor didn't want us to put her back on the streets, especially as she had featured on a news programme as being a local feral dog, responsible for a fair proportion of the district's street dog problem. It was a total palaver. It took several months of us hiding her until things calmed down. Now, the local people are very happy that she lives with us, safe, with her puppy-rearing days behind her.

Once wonderful Roshy had helped Bonnie to get over her fears, she became his wife and they were inseparable. I couldn't bear to think how one of them would cope without the other. We estimated Bonnie's date of birth to be somewhere towards the end of 2011, and Roshy, we simply couldn't say. All we could do was hope they had a long and happy time together.

Anthony opened the door, causing mass excitement from the dogs inside the house who hadn't seen him for about ten minutes – all except Bonnie, who looked thoroughly annoyed with him. 'We've got a call. A village a few kilometres away has a starving dog running around. I've got the details. You ready?'

'Yeah, the coffee can wait.'

I followed Anthony outside across the courtyard to the pickup. The capture kit was always in the back, along with some packets of wet food and a bag of dry food. It saved time loading and unloading if we knew it was always topped up.

'At least it's stopped raining,' I said as we bumped slowly down the driveway. 'And the track's not been washed away.'

'Never mind our track; if this rain keeps up, the roads are going to wash away,' said Anthony. 'I wouldn't be surprised if there's more rain coming. All part of the joy of dog rescue.'

'Who doesn't love the smell of wet dog?'

'Perhaps we could branch out – you know, scented candles, room spray.'

'Eau de Rex? A little dab behind the ears.'

Twenty minutes later we found the village, but not the dog. Perhaps the rain had forced him to take shelter somewhere. It was a typical small village with only a couple of roads and a smattering of houses, some barns and lots of open space. We peered over a few walls, into gardens and checked the barns and garage doors to see if they were open. Nothing at all.

When we had looked absolutely everywhere, we decided to call it a day and head home. As we did so, we saw a medium-sized tan and black dog standing by the side of the road. 'That's him,' said Anthony.

'I'll go,' I said as he pulled over.

I got out and Anthony stayed in the truck. Sometimes, dogs are better with women than they are with men. I crouched down, a packet of food in my hand, ready to offer some to the visibly hungry dog. He started to step towards me, ears back, tail between his legs, but he seemed more intent on the food than anything else. As I started to make friends with him, I heard something in the long grass by the side of the road. Hidden in the grass was another dog. This one was lying on his side, looking up at me. All I could think was how much bigger the dog's head was compared to his neck. At least he was alive and moving. If it hadn't been for the tan and black dog, we would never have found the second dog.

We went home that day with two dogs instead of one. We called the black dog in the ditch Benny No Neck. When he stood up, he was so squat in the shoulders and neck, he reminded us of Grant Mitchell. We had no idea how much of an impact Benny No Neck was going to have on us and Street Hearts. Poor Benny.

21.

Good Days and Bad Days

Anthony – Then – September 2018

It turned into quite the year; some of it was good, some of it wasn't. Throughout the time we've been here, trying to save dogs' lives, there have been moments when I felt like jacking it in. Mainly when we've had problems from the hunters, or dogs have been found poisoned, or people have driven at our dogs. We've had the Food Standards Agency investigate us because of complaints that have been lodged about us and police reports that third parties have instigated. These people have come to our property and caused us issues there; it has never been the other way around. In a bid to help us explain what we were doing, the municipality arranged for us to do a short documentary to go out on Bulgarian television one Saturday morning primetime slot in May 2018.

The day before, we had had so many problems with people in town, I rang the municipality and told them that I wasn't doing the interview. How could I be positive on TV when I'm getting all this crap from people in town? All Emma and I were trying to do was help. 'It's not a request, I'm absolutely not doing it,' I said.

When Emma and I got back from walking the dogs there was someone outside the gates. He turned out to be the municipality mediator; I didn't even know they had one. His remit was to persuade us to do the publicity for the sake of the greater good. And to be honest, he was right, but I wasn't in the right frame of mind following the relentless hostility we faced from some local people. We didn't get any positive response from the TV broadcast, but it didn't do us any harm either. I told Bulgaria that Little Blackie sleeps on my bed, as well as the pitiful story of how Big Lad came to live with us. The main outcome of the feature was that many more people knew where to dump their dogs in the future and brought them to the bottom of our lane. When the presenter was interviewing us for the programme, she asked the question, 'Do you ever feel like giving up?' I said, 'Yes, yesterday.'

As the year went by, it was as if the weather was matching our mood. The rain didn't let up and the storms and floods got worse. Eventually the torrential rainstorms resulted in the lanes in the village getting trashed, bridges were demolished and there were forest landslides. Tragically, people were killed; it was absolutely terrible. As we had the digger and machinery, someone in the village visited us and asked if we'd help repair the lanes. Of course, the answer was yes: we wouldn't have done anything else. We not only had the equipment to do it, but a safe descent into Glushka via the track I'd spent days adopting and resurfacing.

Emma and I went into the village with the tractor on our trailer. The devastation was immediately obvious from the metre-deep trenches in the gravel, to the landslips where the gravel had been washed to the bottom of the hills. It was an awful sight. Our house hadn't completely escaped the deluge either. Some friends of Emma's were staying with us, so we left them to mop out our house, with a promise that we would be back soon to help them.

There are two entrances to our village, and one is more densely populated than the other. The one that Emma and I usually use is the less populated of the two. We agreed to do the decent thing and went to the other side first, straight down the hill. We loaded the gravel from the bottom of the hill and put it on the trailer. Then we drove it back to the top of the hill where it belonged and went back and did it all again. It took us something like twenty loads. Once we had tipped all of the gravel back to where it should have been throughout the village, we returned with the digger to level it out. Everyone was out with rakes and brushes helping; it was a real communal event. When that side was completed and it came to doing the same on the other side of the village where Emma and I live, everyone disappeared. Emma and I had to do it all ourselves. We had spent so much of our time helping and trying to do good, but when the villagers had what they wanted, they disappeared. A local newspaper got wind of the story and put photos of us in the paper, the article detailing the English people who did a great thing for the village.

By now, we had received the fantastic news that we had been granted our shelter licence, so there was little to stop us making the adoption side of things really work. We were now a fully licensed private dog shelter with fully licensed vehicles to operate within Bulgarian law and the European TRACES system, which is the certification platform that allows us to legally move the dogs. Yes, we still seemed to be picking up endless starving and neglected dogs from the side of the road and behind buildings, inside litter bins and anywhere else people thought it was a good idea to leave them, but at least we could go full steam ahead into finding them new homes.

The transformation involved meeting after meeting with a wealth of officials. We needed planning permission to turn our property from domestic to business use, and happily we had already had the access lane surveyed and mapped. It still meant that we had numerous visits to the notary for various legal documents. Our registered NGO had to be formed through the lawyers and courts, plus three visits by the state vets to us and three visits by us to them. The old ramshackle potting shed where we had first put Tipsy on her late-night arrival was now the clinic, a space for postmortems and veterinary treatments. There were so many protocols and documents produced in relation to operating a rescue shelter; we had had no idea when we started out how much was involved. We were required to have a quarantine area which then needed official approval. Plus, we needed an official contract with our vet, a contract with a registered pest control company – the list went on. And still, the dogs kept coming.

Somehow we managed to get it all done, in amongst continuing our ever-increasing daily chores, continuously improving our facilities and maintaining regular neutering. When Emma and I take a moment – if we ever get one – to look back at everything, we're not really sure how we did it. But we did.

Sadly, we realised that neutering and rescuing dogs was never going to be enough and we needed an education programme, as well as open days at Street Hearts. We needed to teach people that it wasn't OK to chain up a dog and never let it move more than a metre or so, the importance of neutering, feeding dogs the correct food (not bread), and caring for them as living creatures. Even so, we felt that the message was beginning to get out there amongst the younger generation if nothing else.

It had taken us over a year and half to get to this stage and involved an enormous amount of fundraising. The list of people who helped us is a vast one, but during 2018 alone so many did so much for us. Mandie Appleby, an expat who lives in the region, organised a crowdfunder which paid for us to build a doggy play park. This massively helped both us and the dogs. The British residents of Slaveykovo and the surrounding villages raised money between themselves to help neuter dogs in their area. Our friend Jane Duberley organised a race night which was an enormous success, and the money raised enabled lots of local dogs to be neutered. The wonderful Pauline and Andy Trent, who live in Bulgaria, have continued to take part in car boot sales to raise money for neutering street dogs and cats. The two of them have also held raffles and arranged discos and other social functions for us too.

Vonnie Young, another expat who lives in Bulgaria, very kindly decided to paraglide off the cliffs of Skalsko in aid of Street Hearts. It was a hugely successful day in Skalsko village centre which had a fantastic turnout of both British and Bulgarian people, along with four local mayors attending. More important than anything else was the 4,000 leva (£1,800) Vonnie raised for us. The money was put to good use, and we immediately spent some of it on medication. Rabies vaccinations, eyedrops and tubes of tranquilliser paste were the very first purchases – all essential items.

Without the support from those who have adopted the dogs we rescue, neuter, give medical treatment to and train, we wouldn't get very far at all. When we see dogs go to their new homes and have the lives they deserve, it makes us so happy and a touch emotional at times. These dogs deserve the best, and with our adopters' help, they get it.

As sad as it can be when the dogs leave us, it also frees up our time to go out and neuter more dogs. This is essential in reducing the unwanted dog and puppy population, as well as those same animals being abandoned on the streets.

Our network of fosterers was growing and took on dogs when we were at capacity. If that wasn't enough, we had volunteer after volunteer who wanted to come out and work with us. We received the great news that Dan Gorman wanted to come back for a second stint. Neither Emma nor I had to think about it twice. We were looking forward to welcoming him back to our shelter.

22.

What's Bulgarian for Broken Neck?

Emma – Then – September 2018

Dan was back with us for a week and a half. Generally speaking, we preferred volunteers to come out for at least two weeks. It takes them a while to get into the routine of everything and to fully understand what is required of them and what to expect. Dan was clearly different as he had been with us only a year before. It was still great having him here, but the time rushed by, and then he was getting ready to leave again. Anthony was busy building the pens and putting up fences, assisted at times by Dan, but quietly getting on with it, as he does. By quietly, have I mentioned the number of times that Anthony tells me how resourceful he is? If he's told me once, he's told me a hundred times. Dan smiled every time I shouted at Anthony to look out, watch what he was doing or get down off the roof.

'I'm all right,' Anthony called down to me from the apex of his old workshop while I looked nervously up at him. 'I know what I'm doing.'

'It doesn't take skill and talent to fall and break your neck.' I watched Dan from the corner of my eye as he left us to it and walked into one of the completed dog runs to sit with some of the more nervous dogs for an hour or two. He clearly didn't want to witness Anthony plummeting to his death. He had a plane to catch.

'It's not the first time you've done something that stupid,' I said, not wanting to have a row when my husband was six metres off the ground, but unable to stop myself. 'Health and safety means nothing to you. The first year we were here, you insisted on going down the well to fix the pump. We had no idea how deep it was and I begged you not to. I couldn't even speak Bulgarian back then, so calling an ambulance would have been interesting. You wouldn't listen to me.'

'I'm listening to you now, aren't I?' Anthony peered down at me. 'I'm a captive audience on this roof. You've waited until I'm on the roof to have a go at me for not taking care. Can you see the irony?'

'I begged you not to tie the strap around the back of the truck and lower yourself into the well. I was hysterical.'

'You were overreacting, just like you are now.'

'If you'd fallen down that well, I wouldn't have got you out and I wouldn't have known who to call,' I said, shielding my eyes from the late afternoon sun as I stared up at him.

'At least you know people now,' said Anthony as he stepped from one part of the roof to another. 'And you know all the Bulgarian words for fall *and* broken neck.'

'You're so funny.'

'You know how I feel about these things,' he called down to

me as his foot slipped. My heart was in my throat, then he righted himself again. 'I'd rather burn out than fade away.'

'I'm going to talk to Dan,' I said. It was probably better that I let Anthony get on with it. Besides, I'd hear the noise of the fall and he was quite right: my Bulgarian really was much better now.

'You all packed and ready for the morning?' I said to Dan through the fence. He sat on a tyre with one of the puppies in his lap and another two rolling around next to his feet, their tiny bodies creating a small dust cloud.

'Yes, I'm packed,' he said. 'It's been great. I'd love to come back and work in Bulgaria at some point in the future.'

'Why don't you live here for a year?' I said. Dan looked stunned. Anthony and I had discussed how much we liked having him around, and besides, the shelter needed good people, and Dan was a good person. We had spent a little over four weeks in each other's company, but we both knew that this was the right thing for Street Hearts, and hopefully Dan would say yes.

I left Dan to it; I didn't want to put him on the spot. I had things to do, including checking Anthony's life insurance, and we had more volunteers arriving in a day or two.

The following day, Dan was gone with a promise to return, the room was ready for our next intake and the online applications for dog adoptions were coming in one by one. Everything was heading in the right direction. That afternoon, we were out in the truck on our way to the supermarket when I received a garbled call from someone at the monastery. It was the same place that we had rescued Cleo from, so another panicked call was likely to mean more animal trauma. Both Anthony and I had a good understanding of Bulgarian until someone speaks to us in a different dialect and it takes us a moment to understand them. One of the words the man kept using was one that neither of us knew. It was a difficult conversation to follow, yet abundantly clear that they had a problem with an animal. We thought it was another injured dog, so with thoughts of a dog in jeopardy, we decided that we should go straight away.

When we got there, a cloaked monk came out and spoke to us, repeatedly using the word that neither of us understood. Due to a fair amount of urgency as he spoke and the absence of the one word that would have made everything fall into place, eventually Anthony said, 'Can you show us the problem rather than telling us about it?'

The monk walked off around the back of the building, gesturing that we follow him. The monastery is a large building with high roofs and a bell tower spread over a vast area. There are a couple of churches and apartments, as well as a small zoo. The monk pointed up towards the top of the first building to where a peacock had settled itself into the valley between two of the roofs.

Almost in unison, Anthony and I said, 'Oh, the word was *peacock*.' Somehow it had got out of its enclosure and was now several metres from the ground. Anthony and I looked at one another, as well as the Street Hearts logo on our T-shirts which clearly showed two dogs, not birds, and then back at the peacock.

Anthony said, 'We're here now, so we'll see what we can do.'

Then the monk said, 'Can you get it down for us?'

'Emma and I can give it a go.'

'Not another roof,' I said, this time in English. 'I've had enough of roofs for one day.'

The monk rushed off, his cloak and robes flowing behind him, and then he reappeared moments later with a ladder. Immediately, I started to panic. 'Really? I can't watch.'

'You'll have to,' said Anthony. 'You're holding the ladder.'

I watched Anthony climb up onto the roof – even higher than the one he had insisted on perching on the day before – only this time, when he got to the top, he ran across the slate-tiled roof to chase a peacock. What could possibly go wrong? Every time Anthony got anywhere near the peacock, it flew to a higher point on the roof. 'If it can fly,' shouted Anthony, 'it can get itself down.' *Then you come down*, I thought.

I watched the peacock go higher and higher, all the time Anthony going higher and higher. By this time, they were both so far from the ground, I could no longer hear the expletives.

After some minutes, Anthony started to make his way back down again. The monk looked a bit disappointed, whereas I must have radiated relief.

'It's a peacock,' said Anthony, now the proud owner of a new Bulgarian noun. 'If it's got itself up there, it'll fly down and go and get its dinner when it's good and ready.'

'But the jackals will get it,' said the monk.

'The jackals won't climb on the roof and get a peacock, will they?' said Anthony. 'Besides, it's getting dark and the tiles are damp, so I'm going to slip. We're going.'

We walked back to the pickup, and now Anthony was safely on the ground, I couldn't resist. 'You gave up easily back there. I thought you'd prefer to burn out rather than fade away.'

'For a peacock? Get over yourself.'

And that was our second trip to the monastery over with, but by no means our final one.

23.

Hungary and Beyond

Anthony – Now

On the road again. We walk the dogs once more before we head towards the Romania–Hungary border – the entire trip involves 180 dog walks, so another ten ticked off the list – clean the crates and after an hour and a half or so, we take off. Our total overnight stay is somewhere around eight or nine hours, depending on the dogs' demeanour. If we need to stay longer to get them settled, we set off later. The only time they react is whenever we open one of the doors. They associate it with something brilliant about to happen, like a meal or a walk.

Each of our vans is licensed independently and has dual licences too. The licences are required for any journey over 8 hours, and we have to stop and rest for at least 9 in every 24 hours. The only part of the trip we're constrained by is our booking on the Eurotunnel. We've never missed one yet.

Pre-Brexit, we had twelve documents for each vanload of twenty dogs we took across to the UK. Following Brexit, we need 260 documents for the same journey, same number of dogs.

There's nothing new on these additional documents: they contain exactly the same information as was contained within the original twelve we used to need. Clearly someone thought that was a good idea.

Problems arise now because there isn't adequate training given to make the French aware of the new UK system. There is the added hindrance of frequent inconsistency with staff who aren't fully up to speed on the documents needed for us to enter the UK with the dogs.

It is extremely rare that we don't get an issue on the final leg of the journey, and while I find puppy farms and dog smuggling abhorrent, this is doing little to stop it. I know that I'm a target because the signage on the van makes it clear who we are and what we're transporting. That expected, yet dreaded, confrontation is still a few days away.

The border between Romania and Hungary looms in the distance. Luck is on our side this morning as we avoid stops and Lauren drives us onwards towards Budapest. There is little movement or noise from the dogs who are at ease with the motion of the bus and hum of the engine as the miles soar past.

Past Budapest towards Bratislava, Slovakia, to another of our regular stopping places where we walk the dogs again. This part of the journey can take four to six hours depending on the traffic, and so it's a good opportunity for more photos on the WhatsApp group, and, of course, for the dogs to get out and stretch their legs. Before we get back in and I take my turn driving, I scroll through my messages to make sure there's nothing I need to take care of, and no impending disasters when we reach our final destination. If there's something that I can lend a hand with, I'm always more than happy to oblige, even if it involves freezing cold nights in South Manchester trying to catch a feral dog.

Back in January 2019, mercifully pre-lockdown, I was on my way to England on a transport run when I was alerted to a missing dog. Friday, a feral dog, had been at Dogs 4 Rescue for some time before, finally, someone took him on as a foster dog. Within days of him getting to his temporary home, he went AWOL. Dogs 4 Rescue spent days helping the foster carers look for him, but he was always one step ahead of them. Despite knowing the dog was running free in the urban outskirts of Stockport and spending nights sat in the woods looking for him, after two weeks they hadn't been able to recapture him.

I was already en route to England on a transport run with a bus full of new adoptees and said that I could spend a couple of extra days helping them to look for the dog before returning to Bulgaria. Dogs 4 Rescue had previously put out an appeal via social media for anyone in the area to contact them. Two women got in touch when they spotted a dog in their garden that they thought was Friday. Their house backed on to some woods and he was managing to get into their garden via a broken fence panel. They left food for him and contacted the fosterers, who in turn asked me to help out.

Fortunately, the homeowners were extremely obliging and allowed me – along with a lot of help from Lou who worked at Dogs 4 Rescue – to turn their thirty-metre by ten-metre back garden into a dog trap. We had to make sure he couldn't get out – this was a feral dog, so I was taking no chances he'd be able to run off again – though it had to be non-scary, so it didn't frighten him. The wooden fence panels were slotted into the posts but were only four to five feet high. We used temporary fencing and wire mesh to raise the height to ten feet and used a rope attached to the panel where he was getting in. We rigged up cameras in the garden and garage and, along with the metal grates and huge magnets I had in my van, we turned the whole garden into a trap cage. The trap door itself relied on two magnets attached to the bottom of it so it would slam shut. The door was propped open with a piece of wood, and from the wood we fed the string through the garden into the garage.

Once it was set up, Lou and I went back in the snow to recapture Friday. I was in place in the garage keeping a careful watch on the cameras, ready to pull the trap cord. I could see that the dog was partial to Peperami, but he wasn't venturing far enough into the garden for me to pull the cord. He stayed too close to the gate to risk me pulling it and either scaring him or injuring him.

It was a long, sleepless night in the snow before Friday eventually came far enough past the boundary. It felt as though I'd been sitting still for hours when he finally jumped down onto the decking, away from the trap door. I pulled the cord to trap him in the garden, except the noise and movement of the gate falling into place against the magnet startled him. We ran to the gate, Lou lost her footing and slipped, and I kicked the cameras over in the tumble. As we crashed around in the garden, the very anxious Friday bolted. He found the only exit – he ran into the garage and hid under a speedboat that was stored in there. Exhausted and relieved, we crawled under the boat to get him and return him to his foster home. The whole incident added four nights to my trip, every cold night worth it.

I finish checking my messages – happily no dogs missing in action – and then we're off to Czechia. It's not a hard border, but, again, sometimes we're stopped, other times we're not. The route we are about to take is close to Prague, where we plan to stop in a town called Plzeň, which in English translates to 'Pilsner'. For some reason, it's always a few degrees colder in Czechia than Hungary. Not that the dogs will be at all bothered by the drop in temperature. They still get their walk at the large service area where we park up and feed them before it's time to call it a night.

Lauren and I also benefit from being able to take it in turns to make use of the service station showers, one of us staying with the bus and dogs at all times. It's still many more hours of driving before we'll finally get time for sleep.

24.

Renée the Rescued Dog

Anthony – Then – April 2019

Several years after Emma and I started the shelter, we thought that we had seen it all. From Tipsy crawling out of a pile of rubbish in the middle of the night, Big Lad getting a beating and being left to starve to death in a locked shed and Cleo's collar embedded centimetres into her neck, we thought that the horror might stop, or at the very least, stop shocking us to the core. It didn't.

It had only been three months since we had been called to a house in Dryanovo where the owner had passed away, apparently leaving four dogs behind. The authorities had taken his body, but left his pets in the house.

With snow on the ground, we went into a single-storey house, the dirt and squalor making breathing a chore. Old clothes, black bags of rubbish, broken furniture and filth greeted us everywhere. One old dog shuffled off as we moved through the debris while a skinny cat stared at us. Another dog had already starved to death on the floor in what was the living room, bedroom and kitchen. Down in the basement was the body of another dog that had been partially eaten. I knew that there was a fourth dog somewhere. It took me some time until I found her squeezed into a box barely large enough to contain her. How petrified she must have been to squeeze herself inside, I couldn't imagine. She was the only one who made it out alive. The other dog and the cat were in such an awful state, the kindest thing was to have them put to sleep. We named the surviving dog Hope and took her home. I could tell by her eyes that this was a dog we could help. Her tail wagged for a few seconds as I carried her to the pickup, and then, once inside the crate, she shook uncontrollably. It was one of the worst cases of human and animal neglect that we had ever seen – at that point, anyway.

Somewhere in the run-up to the Easter weekend, we received a phone call from the mayor of Gostilitsa village. She telephoned to say that a French woman had let her know she had seen some dogs on chains and was throwing food over the fence to them and taking them straw to sleep on. Without hesitation, we were ready to go and see what we could do to help.

We knew that we might have to gain entry to premises, and this is something we can't do without a representative from the local municipality with us. Nadia, the local mayor, came with us. The sight that greeted us was something that mortified her, and I won't forget in a hurry.

As I drove along the road to where the house was, a low brick wall on either side of the road marked the boundary of gardens and fields. On one side, a high metal chain-link fence served to keep both trespassers out and prisoners in.

The information passed to us was that there were six dogs at the premises, all of them chained, all of them starving, and some weren't moving. I slowed the pickup as we got near to the house, a typical one-storey stone building fifty metres or so in front of us. Halfway between our truck and the house, a skinny hunting dog, its brown, black and white coat stark against the lush green strip of kerbside grass, had collapsed. We jumped out of the pickup and approached her carefully, her brown eyes flickering towards me as I picked her up. Somehow this remarkable girl had managed to get out of the house and with her final reserve of energy had made it to the roadside and was now dying of starvation. Probably too weak to object, she didn't make a sound or move as I put her in the truck. She was clearly breathing, but that was about it. She lay in a crate, the rise and fall of her chest reassuring us that she was going to make it. One dog safe, five to go.

It definitely got tougher from then on.

I went inside the house and out into the garden, municipality representatives close by. There were five more dogs chained on the premises; sadly, one had already starved to death, its body starting to give off a pungent odour. The rest of the dogs were secured too far apart to give them a chance to eat it. That left four for me to deal with. Equally as upsetting as the one that had died of starvation, if not more so, was that one of the others was so far gone, it had clearly lost its mind.

I've seen this before with starving dogs – they are past the point of no return and we can't bring them back. We have tried and tried in the past, which gives you some indication of how pitiful this problem is and how it's been wading through this mire. When we see it in the dog's eyes, we know it. It's so incredibly upsetting, but the dog had started to charge at everything around it. He had attacked a number of other dogs. We can't leave any dog to injure humans or other animals when it's been driven insane by being imprisoned and starved to the brink of death. The kindest and safest thing was to put the dog to sleep. An awful decision, and not one that anyone wanted to make.

Another of the dogs we managed to save was a striking-looking beast, despite her being only about a week away from starving to death. Her face and chest were white, her ears and body were black, her legs brown and one of her eyes blue, while the other was brown. She had the saddest, but kindest face. Another hunting dog left to starve. We had been repeatedly told by municipality officials that hunting dogs were always well cared for by their owners. If chaining dogs up until they starve to death was how hunters took care of them, no wonder there were so many unwanted dogs on the streets.

With ill-disguised contempt for whoever had left these dogs to die, Emma and I took the four who could be saved back to Street Hearts. We didn't know how things would work out for them, but we wouldn't stop until we had found them wonderful new homes. We left a very furious mayor at the house. Nadia was determined to pursue the matter and make sure whoever had done this was not going to get away with it.

At least there was some justice: the man who owned the house in Gostilitsa where we found the dogs was prosecuted and banned from keeping animals. Tragically, we met him on another occasion when we had cause to visit him and his dogs on his farm. That wasn't a particularly happy tale either …

We gave the rescued dogs French names in honour of the lady who found out about the dogs and managed to get word to us. The starving dog I picked up by the roadside we called Renée, and the striking dog with one blue and one brown eye we called Phoebe. At least their stories have a happy ending.

25.

Did You Say Cats?

Emma – Then – May 2019

It had been a trying few months. We were taking in dog after dog, some needing much time and attention, such as Hope; some adjusting easier, like Phoebe and Renée. We were relieved that they made full physical recoveries. Their mental state would take a little longer, but both were remarkable girls and came on in leaps and bounds.

Kate had been to stay with us again – always a wonderful time for us – and if that wasn't enough, Dan Gorman had left his job in Devon, packed up his car with his belongings and travelled back to Street Hearts. We had told him that the journey would take him about five or six days. Dan explained that he had never driven abroad and certainly had never embarked on a drive close to 2,000 miles to get somewhere. One April afternoon, he reached our gates, still in one piece, although he visibly paled when he spoke of the German Autobahn.

As soon as Dan had unpacked, he was ready to get stuck in. It made such a difference to Anthony and me to have someone around who didn't need everything explaining to them. Dan never once got paid and he never wanted a day off. The shelter is a much better place for having him here. For Dan's prolonged stay, we had given him the caravan for the summer months so he could have time on his own – or with some dogs for company: all of our volunteers end up with several dogs lodging with them at some point in their stay.

I gave Dan a coffee (Anthony had turned him into a coffee snob during his last two visits) and then I asked him to spend some time in one of the pens with several dogs that we were socialising. Every dog varies in how they adapt to being around humans, but the ones I had asked Dan to check on were slowly getting there. A couple of times I walked past and he was happily playing with the dogs. It felt as though he had never left.

An hour or so later Dan came out and asked me if there was anything else I wanted him to do. 'How were the two ginger dogs?' I said. He looked puzzled. 'Shandy and Sherry? They've been here about a month now but both of them are still very shy.'

'They must be,' he said. 'I didn't see any ginger dogs. There were four dogs and they all played together.'

'No,' I said, 'there are six dogs in there, and two of them are ginger.'

We walked back over to the pen and two ginger faces popped up from behind a row of tyres. 'They came from a village nearby,' I said to Dan. 'They were absolutely petrified when they got here, so who knows what's happened to them. They're very wary of people and spend most of their time hiding from everyone.'

'Could they be rehomed?' said Dan.

'See what you can do in the next twelve months,' I said. 'Once the next transport trip of dogs leaves, we can move Shandy and Sherry to the yard, get them more used to people.'

Over the coming weeks, I very much left things up to Dan with these two beautiful, yet petrified dogs. Each was about the size of a beagle with tan and white markings, their brown eyes wonderfully warm, yet wary. I watched as day after day, Dan and the inseparable dogs bonded. He interacted with them, trying to reduce their anxiety. They would still run or find a corner to hide in, and as Dan approached them, the dogs would sometimes shake in fear and curl up tightly together. Everyone hated to see them in such a state, but Dan took it slowly and tried time and again until they started to relax. I had a very good feeling that these lovely girls would one day find new homes.

Eventually both dogs became very playful with the other dogs. One day I witnessed a breakthrough when they jumped in excitement as I passed by their pen. Dan was behind me with a bag of treats and both girls wagged their tails in excitement as he reached their gate. I couldn't tell you how happy that made me. I didn't have to ask Dan if he was pleased with their progress – it was written all over his face.

As I marvelled at this development, Anthony appeared at my side. He was no doubt taking a break from trying to get run over by his own tractor – I've lost count of the number of times he's managed to roll it while still on it. 'You're doing a grand job there, Dan,' he said.

For a minute or so, the three of us took in the sight of Shandy and Sherry exhibiting happy behaviour, thanks to Dan.

'I've been meaning to ask you,' said Dan, as he bent down to stroke Sherry's head. 'I know that it's predominantly about dogs in the shelter, and that's why I'm here. However, as you know, I love cats; they are my number one animal. I got my first cat when I was sixteen or seventeen and until I came out here, I've had one ever since. Is there any way, if, while working here, I could set about getting the street cat population under control?'

'Fine by me,' I said.

'Of course,' said Anthony. 'You know we'll support you in any way we can.'

'I thought that I could do much the same as you're doing with the dogs,' said Dan. 'I can trap, neuter and return the cats.'

'It's a good plan,' I said. 'You'll need somewhere to keep them. How about the room above the stable?'

'Thank you,' he said. 'That's ideal. I'll buy some equipment, clear out the room and once I've caught the cats, they can stay there overnight before I take them to be neutered at the vet's the next day.'

That was exactly what Dan did. And he did it tirelessly with as many cats as he could find and afford to fund.

Dan Gorman, volunteer

Even though I had been at the shelter working with the dogs twice before, I had lots to learn, such as lead training and how they interact with each other. I saw some sad cases, the worst of humanity. Where I lived in Devon was quiet, with little obvious signs of animal abuse and neglect. This was very much on the front line and was quite an eye-opener. The dogs that come into Street Hearts are broken, both physically and mentally. The resilience of Emma and Anthony is the main factor in the rehabilitation of these damaged dogs.

In my first week or two of moving out there, in April 2019, we got a report of a very sick dog that had given birth to a litter of puppies. We made our way to the outskirts of Dryanovo towards the house where the dog was. A woman brought out an adult dog to meet us. She had her arms wedged under the dog's front legs with the dog hanging down towards the ground. I can still picture it so clearly, and how half-dead the dog seemed. We took the dog, not sure whether she was going to make it, and then focused on finding the two puppies that were behind the house somewhere.

The sight that greeted us was a seven-foot-high pile of scrap metal, wood, fabric and other general rubbish where the two puppies were hiding. We rooted around in the mess and eventually located them.

We called them Bugsy and Spike, and their mum, Tilly. The puppies seemed fine, and promptly adjusted to their new living accommodation, before being quickly rehomed. Tilly, happily, made a full recovery although she took a little longer.

I was initially living in the caravan on the edge of the Street Hearts' shelter so took Tilly with me. I spent that summer with a scared dog, helping her get better. She became my 'caravan dog'. Once Tilly was ready to leave us behind, I was fortunate enough to be on the transport run that took her to Dogs 4 Rescue in Manchester, where she too was rehomed quite quickly. Tilly will always have a special place in my heart, as she went from being so close to death to being my favourite dog.

I am very grateful to Emma and Anthony for enabling me to spend time on the cats, as this was time I didn't spend with the dogs. One day I was out in the forest trapping cats to take to the vet for neutering. I had three spaces and already had two cats, leaving room for only one more. I saw two more cats walking towards me and that one of the cat's ears were red-raw from scratching. I was praying that he would be the one to go inside the trap, as it was obvious that he was in desperate need of treatment. Luckily, he obliged.

The veterinary assistant said that she had never seen a cat with so many fleas. The fleas had caused the cat to scratch behind his ears to the point of making them bleed. Although the cat was very friendly, he was also weak, prompting me to want to keep him for a couple more days. That was the point when I knew that I couldn't let him go. He was the most amazing cat, around fourteen or fifteen years old and black in colour. I decided to call him Flea and kept him with me. Flea made himself at home around the shelter and wasn't in the slightest bit scared of the dogs. He was so comfortable around them that we made him the shelter's cat-friendly tester. It's important that the dogs Street Hearts rehome have been tested around cats if the adopter already has a resident cat. The website is updated with dogs waiting to be adopted and each dog's general information lets the would-be adopter know whether the dog has spent time around cats. If testing hasn't been carried out, it can be on request.

Flea was a lovely cat and although I hated to leave him behind when I returned to England, he was too old to come with me. The move and journey would have been too much. He stayed at Street Hearts where Emma and Anthony looked after him until he passed away in 2022.

26.

Happy Dog Tails

Anthony – Then – November 2019

In amongst the daily heartache and sadness of some of the dogs we rescued, we were rehoming so many that it made it worthwhile. The first two dogs we sent to the UK were Dimitar (named after our vet) and Maria. They went off on a Bulgarian transport company to Dogs 4 Rescue in Manchester. We knew that they would be well cared for and sent to superb homes, but it didn't stop Emma crying with worry as they went on their way. I was pretty choked up about it too.

Dimitar was such a tiny puppy Emma couldn't stop thinking about him. Maria was a Westie-type who had been riddled with mange when we found her before we nursed her back to health. After Dimitar and Maria, we worked closely with Dogs 4 Rescue for some years. Now, however, we rehome all of our dogs direct to owners and have established ourselves a terrific network of fosterers who step in if there's a delay in taking one of the dogs, or something unavoidable happens to the new owners. This avoids any of them spending more time in another rescue centre, no matter how excellent the set-up.

Whenever our dogs leave us, we still have a twinge of sadness to see them go. It's a happy occasion, but we still think about them all.

It's this hope for the dogs' futures that drives us to get out of bed every morning. One of us still asks the other if it's time for bed yet as we wake with the rising sun and birdsong, but get up we do.

Phoebe, the once starving dog I had picked up from the side of the road in Gostilitsa, was with us at the shelter for some time before we could rehome her. Like many of our rescues, it took a tremendous amount of working with her before she could be put up for adoption. When Phoebe was ready, we added her photograph and a bio to our website and had the usual feelings of excitement that someone, somewhere, would get to share their lives with this extraordinary dog.

Along with the 'after' pictures of how Phoebe looked, safe in our shelter and well cared for, we had added 'before' photos. We never want or aim to shock anyone, only to inform and raise awareness of what we are up against. When we rescued her from the awful conditions she was enduring, she was skin and bones; her weight was around 11 kg, which is far from a healthy weight for a dog of her size. Phoebe's story and pictures struck a chord with Lisa Haslinger in Vienna. Lisa and her ex-girlfriend had found out about Street Hearts through a Viennese influencer, followed us on social media and fallen for Phoebe.

There was some stalling before we could finally get Phoebe to Vienna, but once she had her paws under the table in her new home, she couldn't have been more loved and cared for. Lisa and her ex-girlfriend make sure that Phoebe wants for nothing, and we really enjoy getting her updates and seeing her photos.

In November 2019, Dan said that he wanted to come with me on the journey to Manchester, partly because Tilly was going to be on the bus. On this occasion we would visit Dogs 4 Rescue. Their shelter is a similar set-up to ours at Street Hearts: the dogs are free-running and together both indoors and out. This means that if a dog left our shelter and spent any amount of time at Dogs 4 Rescue, it continued to enjoy plenty of space and socialisation. The other two lucky dogs we managed to save from Gostilitsa had already made the journey to Manchester where they were adopted by superb new owners.

This particular visit to Dogs 4 Rescue was a poignant one for Dan. Emma and I tried on many occasions to make Dan cry – he never did – but I really thought the day we waved goodbye to Tilly might be the day.

27.

What Could Possibly Go Wrong?

Emma – Then – March 2020

Dan's final stay with us marked the beginning of the positive changes we needed at the shelter. When 2019 and swine flu were finally behind us, we thought that 2020 was going to be an extraordinary year. It had started well: in February, Dan and I attended a course at Battersea Dogs and Cats Home in London. This completely life-changing experience was the turning point for the shelter.

The course helped me to focus on what we wanted from the volunteers and to structure their time here. We needed to let them know the rules and the ins and outs of what was being asked of them. I had previously attended a course at the Dogs Trust in 2017. Looking back, I don't think that we were quite ready to incorporate everything I'd heard on the Dogs Trust course at the time. I found some of it overwhelming and doubted my own ability. By the time I went to Battersea, it was definitely a different story. Battersea's grants manager spoke to us on the course about applying for funding, and we were given invaluable advice on what our shelter intake should be, what sort of dogs we should take on, how to assess their behaviour, what the recruitment process for the volunteers should be and how to work out a robust adoption process.

Things really started to adapt into a totally different set-up once Dan applied for a £10,000 shelter improvement grant, approved and agreed by Battersea. It enabled us to take care of the drainage; improve the ark (a former shed that now holds around fifteen dogs); gravel the communal areas which had always been boggy and prone to spreading infection; install hygiene stations for cleaning the dog mess scoops; and put in an open-sided staff kitchen for preparing the dogs' meals, medication, and grooming. It was a lot of money and we put every last pound to full use. To fill up the water bowls and buckets, we had got used to dragging a hosepipe 200 m several times a day. It was inefficient and took up so much time. Now, we had a water station, saving us hours.

It wasn't only the physical environment that the course changed for the better. The volunteer recruitment process got a shake-up of epic proportions. It was clear to applicants that if they wanted to be prospective volunteers, they should only apply if they were willing to perform. If they weren't able to give that reassurance, they wouldn't get through the paper sift. We got our act together in spectacular style. We started a database called Shelter Manager that we use to store details of all of the dogs' medication, any information about their behaviour, where they came from and when they arrived at the shelter and where they were rehomed to.

The Battersea course gave us an insight into what they do, how they work and what their policies are. We were joined by people from the UK, Cyprus, India and Romania. It was reassuring to hear that their processes were like our own and that we knew we weren't alone in what we were trying to achieve.

In early spring 2020 Anthony and I planned a transport run to England. One of the dogs who had gone on the last run was Bizzy Lizzie, a Garden of Doom dog. She had been living with us since her rescue in 2016 and the Street Hearts shelter was becoming too much for her. While we thought that, as a much older dog – she was around eight years old at this time – she would live out her days with us, we knew that the best thing for her was to take her to Dogs 4 Rescue. They have such a wide range of potential adopters, we knew that someone would take care of her. Bizzy Lizzie had shown us just how tough she was when we found her in the Garden of Doom, so I had every faith things would work out for her. I was delighted when I found out that an older man, in his seventies, had really taken to Lizzie. Apparently the feeling was mutual as she tried to climb on his knee. He took Lizzie home with him on foster trial, and what should have been the beginning of a long and happy pairing unfortunately was anything but. In the run up to the first lockdown in March 2020, this now distraught gent brought Lizzie back to Dogs 4 Rescue. He was heartbroken but said that lockdown meant that he wouldn't be able to walk her. He had been walking miles with her every day, but because he was in the age bracket for locking down early and having to avoid people, he made the crushing decision to give her up.

Our friend Jane Duberley had posted about Lizzie on our Facebook page, where she caught the eye of Mel and Phil Oyston. Lizzie has gone on to have the most incredible life and is now cared for by two wonderful adopters. I thought it only fair to warn Mel and Phil before they took Lizzie on that she could be cantankerous at times. The last thing I wanted to do was to bring a dog – any dog – back to Bulgaria, but it crossed my mind at one point that it might be the best thing to do if no one wanted a grumbly dog in her later years.

In the meantime, Covid was sweeping the world and Anthony and I were trying to get back to Bulgaria. Travel restrictions were being imposed, making the journey extremely difficult. As if that wasn't bad enough, Dan was in the shelter on his own with more than sixty dogs to look after. We spoke to him on the phone, where his mild panic was obvious. None of us knew whether it might take weeks or even months for us to get home. There were no other volunteers at Street Hearts at the time, meaning a lot of work for the eight or nine days we should have been away, let alone a lot longer. Our fabulous friend Jane Duberley offered to help out in any way she could. She saved the day for the dogs and Dan by bringing food shopping and going to the shelter most days.

When at last we made it through the door, Dan greeted us with, 'Thank God you're home! I'm not sure how I would have coped. The amount of work is insane.'

Fortunately for the shelter, lockdown was about to ease the workload in the very welcome form of a new team member.

Mel Duff and Phil Oyston in Manchester

When Lizzie, our potential new foster dog, was brought out to meet us, if I'm honest, she looked a bit old and lardy. I remember thinking that I had never seen a dog as frightened as she was. She just hit the floor. She was cowering, avoiding looking at us and wouldn't come near us. When trying to bond with a foster, we would usually walk the dog down the lane beside the shelter and offer them a treat. We tried to, but Lizzie wouldn't take it. I remember thinking 'fat little wet Lizzie'. She was so timid. But after forty-five minutes or so, she finally crept over towards us.

This was 18 March 2020, right before lockdown. Phil and I thought, OK, we'll take her for one week and see how it goes. In the meantime, millions of people's lives were about to change drastically, and I found myself one of the many people now working from home. One benefit that came from the huge alterations in our routine was that we bonded with her. So, we held on to Lizzie throughout that period.

By this time, we were probably Lizzie's last chance: she had been an abandoned dog living in the shadow of a derelict house, she was getting on in years and her foster placement had failed. We knew from Dogs 4 Rescue that when she was at the shelter with other dogs, free-running and part of a pack, Lizzie behaved like a normal dog. So Phil and I knew what we had to do for Lizzie – we needed to press the reset button. She could come through this, all she needed was lots of love, time and work. Slowly but surely, we started to get somewhere with her. Then the Thursday night clapping for NHS staff on the doorstep started and the noise set her off. House-training had never been an issue until the clapping started. We were back to the beginning.

We talked about the pluses and minuses of keeping Lizzie and hated the idea of giving up on her. She had already been through so much. Emma had prepared us for Lizzie's potentially grouchy demeanour. By the time she came to live with us, she had shut down so much that Emma had even thought about having her brought back to Bulgaria, where she could live out her years at Street Hearts. We were her last resort. How could we turn her away after all she had been through?

After a month, we got the official adoption and within three months she had already travelled with us to visit my family in Ireland, to Yorkshire and on visits to a beach about an hour away from where we live.

It took Phil and me six months of hard work to get her settled as she was so timid. We took her to our local pub and that proved to be the turning point. Her personality started to come out and has only continued to shine. We then took her to day care where she socialised, and within six months to a year, her personality finally came to the fore.

Lizzie is our first overseas dog, and definitely not the last. In November 2022, we also adopted Dixie from Street Hearts. On occasion we have fostered dogs from Dogs 4 Rescue, and two other dogs from Street Hearts: Wolfie and Hector. What's great is that Lizzie excels at showing other foster dogs the ropes, and even if she shies away from adults, she is great with children. Jane used to call Lizzie 'grandma': Lizzie's granddaughter had puppies in Bulgaria and Lizzie used to look after them, making her a doting great-grandma.

Lizzie learnt to sit on command very quickly. Teaching her was, in some respects, more fun than teaching a dog without her difficult past. She zoomies from time to time, and that's wonderful to see. She's also taken to sleeping in Dixie's crate.

It hasn't all been plain sailing: she's had operations for removal of mammary cancer and lumps removed. She also seems to enjoy mounting other dogs as soon as she gets familiar with them, and mounting them certainly does away with any feelings of shyness or inhibitions. She is definitely anything but a normal dog, which is perhaps not that surprising. She grunts at people – but Emma did warn us that Lizzie was gobby!

Whenever Emma and Anthony drop by on one of their visits to England, Lizzie runs straight up to them. She might grunt and have her ways about her, but she's certainly loyal. Other friends of Emma's who have volunteered at Street Hearts in the shelter have met us, as well as Lizzie.

There's only one Bizzy Lizzie.

28

I Only Came Here to Drop Off a Dog

'Lucy' Lyudmila Krumova, full-time Street Hearts outreach worker

I'm a local so I know the area well. I lived in Dryanovo until I was ten years old when my family moved away. We moved back some years later, and I often walk with my parents in the mountains around here. It was one of these walks in the run-up to Covid that led me to where I am now, living at Street Hearts and working full-time as an outreach worker.

In April 2020, just as Covid was starting, I came back home because everything was closing down and it was impossible to travel from town to town without a valid reason and the correct documents. This decision and enforced situation were totally life-changing for me. It started with a walk in the mountains with my family and a small scruffy dog following us around. I knew about the Street Hearts shelter, so I thought that we could take the dog there and drop her off. Everything was very strict in Bulgaria regarding the measures put in place for Covid so, as we were on our way to the shelter, the police saw us and stopped us. They told us that we couldn't carry on with our journey as Anthony and

Emma had only recently returned from England and had to quarantine for two weeks. I already had a cat and two dogs, so taking in a third dog was going to be very difficult. I kept hold of her for the next couple of weeks until I could get her to Street Hearts.

I really took to the dog. She was three or four months old with long shaggy black fur and a really nice nature, although at that time she was scared. Even so, she still came to me when I called her, and followed us home. I called her Millie.

I then messaged Street Hearts on Facebook to tell them that I had a dog I needed to bring to them whenever I was allowed to pay them a visit. I called Emma and she said that they would take her in a fortnight's time as soon as they were allowed to have contact with people again.

Two weeks went by, and I made my way to Street Hearts to drop off Millie. Naturally, I got chatting to Emma and Anthony and asked them if I could do some voluntary work with them. There was no other local shelter I knew of and it was something that we badly needed in the area. There were lots of strays and so many of them were being poisoned. It was evident that they needed a safe place to be cared for. I started working here around the end of April 2020 and to begin with, I was still living in Dryanovo. I couldn't drive at the time, so I used to cycle to the shelter. It's about eight kilometres each way, taking an hour to get to work and about fifteen minutes back. It's quite an incline to start the day on!

My background wasn't working with dogs, although I had always had a dog, as had my family and friends. My grandma had dogs and chickens and one of her dogs was kept in the house, while the other was kept outside. It wasn't chained up and it was locked in an enclosure at night. There was nothing strange about that, it was how things were. One thing I recall from being a young child in Dryanovo, was that it was full of street dogs. They were never aggressive and didn't attack people – dogs don't tend to do that without a reason – but numerous dogs, on the streets, in derelict buildings or roaming around, is something I have clear memories of. One man who used to be in the area, who was I think homeless, used to go around the bins collecting stuff from them. I remember seeing about ten dogs all around him, as if they were protecting him.

We didn't have a dog shelter in the area, so people who found them a nuisance would take it upon themselves to deal with the situation by poisoning them. Every week I'd see the body of a poisoned cat or dog, dead in the street. They didn't deserve that: they were roaming around, sometimes wanting to play, sometimes simply scared, all because people no longer wanted them. That's not right, when all a dog deserves is a loving home. I once asked my mum why people shouted at dogs and she said that they were taking their own anger out on the animal. Seriously, why do that? It makes me feel bad for the dog. I love all animals so find it difficult to understand.

I found my first dog in Dryanovo when I was eight years old. I cycled home with him and asked my grandma, 'Can I keep him?' She told me to ask my mum and see what she said. My mum said it was OK with her, as long as my grandma gave the go-ahead. I kept my dog and called him Sharo, which means colourful – he was brown, white and ginger. I loved that dog.

My life went on, taking on a vastly different path from that of dogs. I started my studies in science in October 2009 when I moved to Sofia; from there I moved to another town where I then attended a sports school. I was training in judo and sambo, which is a Russian version of Judo. I then wanted a break from competing, so I moved to Moscow for a year. I was training all the while I was in Moscow, but then I came back to the National Sports Academia in Sofia. That was for another four years, so I started up my training again. I really love judo and sambo, but it wasn't the only thing I wanted to do with my life.

As a five-year-old child, I had a dream to have my own dog shelter, with dogs roaming through the forests and not prisoners in the pens. I forgot all about my dream, with life getting in the way, as it does. That all changed when I met Emma and Anthony – my dreams have come true. I know that the shelter isn't mine, but everything here at Street Hearts is good. It's all for the dogs. No other shelter gives their hearts to the dogs like this. I've been to some of the other shelters and they can't compare with what we have here. I know that this is a special place. Even when we go out to catch the dogs, we do it in the least stressful way possible for them. It stops the dogs getting too worried when we capture them and prevents any badly reactive behaviour later on, when we're trying to put slip leads around their necks. By not raising their anxiety levels on capture, they don't associate us taking them to safety with having been handled too excessively or in a heavy-handed manner.

A lot of the problems here relating to our street dogs in Bulgaria are caused by an older generation who think that a dog should be outside protecting their house. The issue I have with that is that the dogs are chained up. A chained-up dog can't protect anything. I know first-hand that some of the older generation of Bulgarians are suspicious of what Anthony and Emma do, largely because they're not Bulgarian and so instinctively don't trust them. There is a feeling amongst some that they breed dogs at the shelter to sell them and make money. That couldn't be further from the truth. The dogs are neutered as soon as they are old enough. There are more than enough dogs to go round, so the last thing we want is even more. Besides, Anthony and Emma came out here to Bulgaria for a nice life, not to fix the mess with dogs throughout the region. Local people complain about the street dogs and then they complain about the very people who are trying to solve the problem they are complaining about. It really makes no sense.

Lauren and I went to Tsareva Livada, a village about fifteen minutes from Dryanovo. We had been told about a dog that had given birth under a bridge, so we went along to try and sedate the dog and bring her and the puppies back to the shelter. A man came out of nowhere and started to accuse us of poisoning the dogs. Where was he when the dogs needed help and feeding? He wasn't interested in that, only in making allegations of something we weren't doing. I told him that we were from Street Hearts and his reply was that the English people were always travelling to the village to poison the dogs. It's so frustrating.

This is only one of the concerns about people and their attitudes towards the dogs. All owned dogs must be microchipped and registered – only there's no consequences if this isn't done. The chipping is never checked and although it can result in a fine, nothing's done about it. Everyone in Dryanovo and Tryavna can take their dog to our local vet Dimitar for microchipping and neutering. It's free for owners: Street Hearts will settle the bill. Still people don't do it. They don't see the point, especially an older generation who keep their dogs on a chain. Their attitude is that the dog can't go anywhere so why bother? There is also a tendency to distrust technology and sometimes it's a cost implication. That's why we cover the costs. Hunters don't like to chip their dogs because they can then throw the dog away if it's no longer any good to them.

We get some friendly dogs in the shelter, and they may be owned dogs, but we can't trace their owners easily. We put the dogs on Facebook, Twitter and other forms of social media, sometimes resulting in people contacting us to say it's their dog. Of course, we then return them, often having treated the dogs for any illness, injury, or sickness, not to mention feeding them well before we give them back.

The biggest problem we face daily is how to accommodate each and every dog. Each one is different. The owned ones that we get from time to time that are subsequently claimed, or the ones that have been someone's pet until they decide to throw them away, are fine with humans. Others get jealous if we stop to stroke another dog; it all depends on the individual – just like humans. If they've been street dogs and then end up here, they don't know that they are safe and out of harm's way. We understand the dog and then they start to show their personality. If they're confident, this naturally takes less time than one that's stressed or scared. Sometimes, although not always, it's the dogs who have been chained up all their lives that show aggression. They are the most upsetting ones.

One such dog is Pikachu. He was a chained dog all his life. Someone who lives and works in Tsareva Livada called me about him. Because Anthony and Emma regularly speak to the mayor and the message is getting out there that I'm the Bulgarian-speaking outreach worker, people often get in touch to ask for my help. This particular woman telephoned me as Pikachu's owner sadly went to hospital and then died. His son lived in Varna and didn't want the dog and didn't want to keep paying someone to go and feed him. We went to get him and he was on a short chain with a bowl of green water. He didn't even have a name at that time. I decided to call him Pikachu. He's a wonderful dog, born around the end of May 2021. He's never shown aggression to anyone, even though he's been kept on a short chain. He's always excited when he goes anywhere, even when we took him to be neutered – not that he knew that, obviously. It was sad that he'd had that start to life, but he adores the daily pack walks with thirty or forty of his close friends.

An owner's reluctance to have their dog neutered is along the same unfathomable lines of thinking. They think if the dog's female then it should have puppies that will help protect the house, and that male dogs will lack the drive to protect the property if they're neutered. It's actually the other way round: male dogs are *more* focused when neutered. Often there is a lack of comprehension about tumours or cancers the dogs are susceptible to if they aren't neutered. It makes sense for so many reasons.

I love my job here as outreach worker, despite the frustrations I've explained. If I could change one thing here in Bulgaria, it would be people's attitudes towards dogs, or, in fact, all animals. The feeling shouldn't be that we are top of the food chain and that nothing else is a human problem. We need to protect everything around us in nature, not just the animals. If my generation thinks like me, and our children and our children's children adopt this approach, things will change. People have a responsibility to care for dogs. These are domestic animals because we have created the problem and now can't choose to turn our backs on it. They don't have a chance to survive without humans. They depend on us for a home, food and water, and everyone needs to know and accept that. A dog isn't trash to throw on the street when you're done with it. They have feelings and emotions – it's a live animal and they suffer physically and emotionally in the same ways as people do.

29

Onwards Through Czechia

Anthony – Now

It's going to take Lauren and me several more hours of driving before we reach our next overnight stop in Czechia. The dogs are settled in their crates, although with a few puppies on board, we may get whimpers and a bit of barking when we try to sleep tonight. It's something that we're used to but doesn't stop us from being woken up more times than we would like. We still have a couple more days and nights to go until we can sleep in a bed that's not on a transport bus, although it never bothers me, and thankfully Lauren has taken it in her stride. Back at Street Hearts, we've learnt that we need to physically shut the dogs in at night to stop them barking. It aids a better night's sleep for us if they're quieter. We need all the energy we can get.

As I've said, we transport the dogs to the UK ourselves now, and this wasn't always the case: early on, we used a Bulgarian transportation company and were in partnership with another rescue charity, but we found that the dogs were not always matched with the most suitable adopters. We knew that this couldn't go on; for one thing, it plays into the hands of those who don't think we should be doing what we're doing.

Once we made the decision to transport and rehome the dogs ourselves, we looked further afield than the UK. We started by contacting over 200 organisations throughout Europe to see if there was demand for adopting any of our dogs. Only one responded: a charity in the South of France who only wanted five dogs every couple of months. That was something that we couldn't commit to, due to the cost implications for such an infrequent and lengthy trip.

Laura Norrey, who works for us full-time in the UK, keeps our Street Hearts website updated with the dogs that are ready for adoption. It sometimes takes weeks or even months before a dog can be rehomed, depending on its background, although puppies are usually easier to find homes for. They don't have the emotional baggage of an abandoned or abused dog, with the exception of slightly older, feral street puppies. Those ones take work, a lot more work, and that involves not only time and money but space in the shelter. For every feral dog we have to rehabilitate, it's taking up the place of so many more.

We can't afford for there to be a space on the transport bus, meaning every trip requires twenty dogs who have had someone see their photos, read their bio and make it through our adoption process. Lauren handles many of these along with Emma, matching each dog to the right home.

The only consistency, throughout our entire Street Hearts' journey, has been a lack of resources. Last year, our vet bill was one hundred and 20,000 leva (£60,000 approximately). We can't reiterate how important our supporters have been in helping us to get where we are today. Each and every person, every single pound, dollar, leva and euro that comes our way makes such a difference, although some people really have gone above and beyond.

Karen Croft, who adopted Rufus after he had recovered from his boar attack, is one such person. Prior to Rufus, Karen and her husband had adopted a dog called Stanley from us. She has also fundraised for us; she has taken care of the signage and window installation for Renée the Rescue Bus; and, in February 2023, raised over £1,000 by donating a prize for two nights' bed and breakfast with dinner for two at her pub the Craven Heifer in Addingham on the edge of the Yorkshire Dales. Emma and I stayed there when we went back to Yorkshire for my dad's funeral. The place was closed for renovation, but Karen being Karen gave us the keys to the top floor which is where the best suites are and said, 'Use the hotel for as long as you'd like.' We can't thank Karen and her family enough for all they've done for us, both personally and for Street Hearts. I know that Karen would dismiss this with, 'It was the least we could do.' The bonus at the end of this trip is that we get to pay her a visit.

Lauren and I clock away the miles, grateful that the snow and ice we frequently get on the winter and spring trips hasn't made an appearance. Much of the journey through Czechia is dual carriageway, so any accident or tailback can result in lengthy delays. At least these dogs are on their way to a better life.

Finally, Lauren and I reach the service stop in 'Pilsner' town in Czechia, where we can walk the dogs and attend to their every need before our own. Shattered, but pleased we've got here in plenty of time for a good night's rest, we call it a day – a very long one – and settle down in our sleeping compartments in Frankie the Furever Bus. I listen to the sound of twenty snoozing dogs about to follow in hundreds of other dogs' pawsteps, the last thing I hear before I drift off.

Karen Croft, supporter, adopter, friend

I've known Anthony and Emma for a number of years now. Whatever they may tell you, I really haven't done that much to help them. You just do your bit, don't you? My husband Phil and I, along with our two sons, have adopted three Street Hearts dogs over the time we've known them. As well as the amazing Rufus, we currently have another three dogs, all rescues. There's a good chance that number will increase. We've never had this many before. Don't tell Anthony and Emma this but we adopted one called Bob from Dogs 4 Rescue. Well, the thing is, Bob came to the UK with Chewie and my husband has fallen for Chewie, so I think he'll be here any moment.

Anyway, I'm skipping ahead. Back in 2016, we were out one evening and chatted with someone who I later friended on Facebook. He then shared some posts about Street Hearts and his wife posted some photographs of a hen do she was at with Emma Smith. Emma's photographs included some of a black and white sheepdog-type dog called Stanley. By the time I made my initial contact with Street Hearts, they had neutered Stanley and released him. I know that they don't do this often now, but at the time, they were still establishing the shelter and without the room and legalities in place, they had no option but to return him to the streets. I told Emma that I'd have Stanley; I'd fallen in love with him.

To begin with, they couldn't find him. They'll tell you themselves that they had to stop capturing, neutering and releasing the dogs as a matter of course, due to the barbaric things some people then did to the released and neutered dogs. Some Bulgarians think it diminishes a dog by neutering it and that leads to poisoning and worse.

Happily, they tracked Stanley down and Emma drove him to Yorkshire so he could come and live with me.

I adored him. He was a super dog. One day, I was out walking him and he simply stopped and sat down. I knew that something wasn't right, so I took him to the vet who checked him out. Initially, he said that Stanley looked fine but when he took his temperature, it was a little on the high side. We keep horses, and sometimes parts of old horse hooves get discarded, so I told the vet that I was worried in case he had eaten some and perhaps it had got stuck somewhere inside his stomach. The subsequent ultrasound didn't show anything so the vet telephoned me and said it may be a good idea if they had a look inside his tummy.

I still can't think about fabulous Stanley without getting upset. The vet called me back to say that Stanley had a perforated stomach. His insides were in a terrible condition and there was a great deal of infection. The operation took seven hours and while they were sewing him up, he died. He didn't make it out of the anaesthetic. I was devastated. Stanley was with us for two years.

About a year after we got Stanley, we adopted Archie from Street Hearts. He was a corgi-type dog and quite a grumpy old man. He must have been nine or ten when a Bulgarian man surrendered him to Emma. The man was moving out of his home and said that he couldn't take the dog with him. He handed over Archie along with a bag of dog food, and then Archie was on his way to Yorkshire. He saw out his days here and, despite his crotchety manner, he had a great time with us.

Street Hearts raised enough funds to buy Renée the Rescue Bus, allowing them to safely bring up to twenty dogs at a time across the continent. They raised the money themselves, but I drove it to a signage workshop on a trading estate in Castleford. A lovely chap sorted it out. I was relieved to get there; I couldn't find the place to begin with and driving, let alone reversing, a vehicle of that size wasn't the easiest. Anything for Street Hearts and I love a project, so it was really no bother at all. Oh, yes, I also arranged to have the back windows installed so that it fully complied with regulations for transportation of the dogs. The left-hand drive headlights needed to be taken care of too. It wasn't a big thing to sort out.

Around this time, one of our sons raised £300 by selling burgers and food at a party he arranged. He wanted to do something to help, so he used the money to buy dog food and loaded it into the van before Anthony drove it back. It also helped to spread the word amongst my son's peer group.

Then, in 2019, along came Rufus, our Street Hearts number three. We've had him about five years now. He's a typical Bulgarian street dog with his black and tan colouring. It's hard to believe how things would have ended for him if Emma and Anthony hadn't found him. Rufus is as soft as butter and follows me around all day. He never does anything wrong; he literally can't do anything wrong. He just wants to please everyone around him and will do anything to oblige. Rufus the amazingly affectionate dog was a snarling mutt at the end of a pole when he first got to Street Hearts.

Emma and Anthony think that Rufus had previously been in a shelter and was then dumped by that shelter. We'll never know, and I can't imagine what he went through. It took Emma and the team years of work to turn him into the docile, loving dog he is now. Emma would lie on the floor with him, feeding him, stroking him, giving him reassurance along with titbits. Years later, their perseverance paid off.

Once he was ready, and not before – that's the special thing about Street Hearts – they sent me lots of photos of him, along with subtle hints, such as 'Look at Rufus!' 'When can Rufus come and live with you?' Anthony and Emma have to keep the dogs moving through their shelter once the time is right. Space is so limited and there are always other animals in need of their help. They knew above all that Rufus would fit in here.

I said yes, and when Rufus arrived from Bulgaria, he came in and jumped straight onto our sofa.

I couldn't imagine life without Rufus. He sometimes gets fearful if there's lots of noise around him. Even though he came to us when he was six or seven, and so is by no means in his infancy, he acts like a much younger dog. He charms everyone he meets, and while he has to trust you, he accepts and loves people. Again, all down to the wonderful job Anthony and Emma do. I think that it broke their hearts a little bit to let him go.

We've always had rescue dogs. I love dogs and grew up with them as a part of our family. They were always dogs that were rehomed by the RSPCA or shelter dogs. I want to help as I know there's a lot of cruelty out there. I struggle to think that animals were treated the same way in the UK sixty or so years ago as they are now in Bulgaria. It's not enough to simply rehome street dogs – people's mindsets must change too.

Emma and Anthony are tidying up the street dog catastrophe so well in their locality, people come from far and near to drop them off. It's understandable that if a place has packs of dogs roaming the streets, the sheer number can make people scared and apprehensive. Street Hearts are trying their hardest to keep it under control. Not for themselves, but for the dogs and for the local community.

Even in the UK, the attitude of some is that dogs from other countries shouldn't be rehomed here. Once they see a healthy, happy dog running around and then find out it's a foreign street dog, and but for Street Hearts and a Brit adopting it, it would be dead, it gives them an entirely different perspective. People can be narrow-minded about such things.

We helped Street Hearts find a facility where they could keep the dogs for forty-eight hours once they come across from Bulgaria. The animals need somewhere to decompress and we were happy to allow them to use a part of an agricultural building we have use of. It's a stable block and not dissimilar to the Street Hearts shelter they have in Bulgaria. They were paying a lot of money for one in Kent, so it was our pleasure to let them use ours. They've given us three wonderful dogs. It seems like a fair exchange.

30.

The Hunters and
the Hunted

Emma – Then – June 2020

It was the usual morning rushing around: Anthony and our newest member of the team, Lucy, were out on the pack walk and I was trying to get some admin taken care of. All the while, I was continually hampered by the dozen or so dogs who opted out of this morning's walk and decided to stop me getting any work done. I've tried to keep the door shut when I'm in my office, but it was futile. At least if the dogs could come and go as they please, they didn't scratch the solid wooden door to pieces as they tried to claw their way to me.

I was lost in thought, and slightly concerned that the mountain of paperwork was going to topple in the warm breeze from the open window, when my phone rang. The noise jolted me from the dog adoption request I was reading.

The screen showed that it was one of the neighbours calling. She lives at the bottom of the hill, at the end of the lane that leads up to our property. She told me that there was a sick dog at the side of the track close to her house. I thought it was a bit strange as our dogs were either on the walk or somewhere around our farmhouse. I went to take a look.

A horrible sight greeted me, something I was truly unprepared for. Benny No Neck, one of our sanctuary dogs, lay dead on the ground. Benny was senior in years, but this was a shock. The only logical conclusion that I could come to was that he took himself off for a walk and had a heart attack. It happens, but this was such a sudden ending for our wonderful boy. I stood for a moment, thinking back to happy times with Benny and how he was the most beautiful soul you would ever meet.

Despite being so upset at the unexpected death of our much-loved dog, I got on with moving him back to the shelter where we could give him a more dignified send-off and get his body out of the increasing warmth of the summer's day.

I knew that Anthony and the rest of the team were going to be mortified at Benny's death, but he was far from the first dog we had lost, and I knew he wouldn't be the last. With heavy feet, I started to walk the kilometre back up the hill.

As I got closer, I heard the sounds of the dogs and humans returning from the pack walk and got ready to deliver the news.

I reached the far side of the farmhouse, through the gate that leads to the puppy runs, and gave a half-hearted wave at Anthony and Lucy as they strolled alongside the chain-link fence. They were flanked by dogs, some hurling themselves down the bank to get back in front of each other. A couple of the puppies went on the walk with them and I momentarily distracted myself from delivering the news of Benny's death by watching them dart into their pens. Hugo, a tan and white three-month-old puppy with big floppy ears, ran into the middle pen. Without any warning, he fell to the ground and stopped moving.

I ran across the gravel pathway, hardly believing what I'd just seen. I got to him at the same time as Anthony and we both checked him for signs of injury.

'He's dead,' I said to Anthony, both of us kneeling beside his tiny body. 'This is the most bizarre thing I've ever seen.'

'What's happened to him?' said Anthony. 'He was fine on the walk.'

I didn't even have time to tell him about Benny, his death now seeming more than a sudden collapse, when I glanced over to where the rest of the dogs were congregating. Panic now gripped me at the realisation that the dogs were moving in towards something on the ground. Please, not another collapsed dog.

'What are the other dogs sniffing at?' I said to Anthony. Before he had a chance to answer me, I stood up and covered the 25 m to where six or seven of them were pawing at the ground.

I shouted to get them out of the way and saw a piece of meat on the floor. I picked it up to stop the dogs from getting it. The chemical smell from the meat was overwhelming.

'It's been laced with something,' said Anthony, as he came to join me. 'I can smell it from here. It looks like chicken, definitely not something that's come from inside the shelter.'

We both peered into the trees lining the sides of the shelter. Our gorgeous home is a sanctuary for the dogs, it's a sanctuary for us, and the feeling that someone was in the forest, watching us, made the hairs on the back of my neck stand up. It was broad daylight, it was a warm and sunny day, yet I could feel goose-bumps on my arms.

'I need to tell you about Benny No Neck,' I said to Anthony, my feelings of concern that we were being watched now replaced with anger. 'He's dead. The neighbour called to say she'd seen a poorly dog at the bottom of the lane. Well, you don't get much more poorly than dead. I thought it was a heart attack, now I very much doubt it.'

'I'm calling the police,' said Anthony, a no-nonsense tone to his voice, probably matching my own, but I was too fired up to care what I sounded like. 'You call the municipality.'

And so we did.

The instruction was to take both Benny and Hugo to a vet in Gabrovo for postmortems. Anthony and I set out in the Toyota, both Benny and Hugo's bodies secured in the back, and drove to the veterinary clinic. As soon as we pulled up into the car park and took a look at the two-storey concrete building, I wanted to believe that I was about to get some answers and find out if we were right about the dogs' unexpected deaths, or whether it was something less sinister. In my heart, I knew that it had to be foul play. I would rather know the truth, even if it was unpalatable.

It started badly; I instinctively knew that it wouldn't get any better. First off, I got a bad feeling from the vet who was oozing attitude from every pore and it was clear to me that he was being made to go through the motions – the bare minimum of motions – and that was as much as he was willing to do. The stocky, dark-haired middle-aged man all but dismissed me, but under the circumstances, I was having none of it. I insisted that I was present when the postmortems took place, which did not go down well at all. I told him in Bulgarian that I used to be a police officer and I knew what to expect. Having seen the process on several people over the years, I'm hardened to it. Dogs wouldn't be any worse.

I met with some resistance, but the vet eventually relented and allowed me to watch the proceedings while Anthony took a seat outside the operating theatre. Before long, the vet pointed at Benny and said, 'This dog died from a heart attack and so has the puppy.'

'Why would a three-month-old puppy have heart disease?' I asked, more incredulity to my Bulgarian accent than Yorkshire twang.

'I'm not sending the organs for toxicology and you can take that meat away,' he said, dismissing me and waving away the box I'd brought the chemical-smelling chicken in. 'It's clearly meat that's had garlic added to it.'

By now, the full extent of just how little this man cared had hit me full on. 'None of us eat meat,' I told him, failing to keep my temper. 'We're vegetarians and don't even have meat on site. How has this got into our shelter? Someone has obviously thrown it in.' I was holding the box towards him, fighting every urge to push it into his pigeon chest. It was clear that I had hit a brick wall with this man.

I was so angry and upset that when I left, I knew that it wouldn't end here. 'We're going to the police,' I told a bewildered Anthony when I came back out to rejoin him.

'That didn't take long. Want to tell me what happened?'

'Pretty much nothing,' I said. 'We're going to the police and we're taking an interpreter with us. I don't want there to be any misunderstandings, or even a hint of a misunderstanding.'

It was a couple of weeks before we managed to get an appointment with the area commander at the police station in Gabrovo. A Bulgarian friend came with us to interpret, and shortly after giving our names at the front counter, the three of us were taken to an office. A tall, authoritative plain clothes officer greeted us and again, despite wanting to do everything properly and by the book, I felt a wave of despair wash over me. He refused to accept that hunters had anything to do with harming our dogs. In fact, this thirty-something-year-old man, immaculate suit, sat opposite us and wouldn't accept that hunters would harm any dog. He told us that the hunters love animal and their dogs. The fact that they go out and shoot animals seemed to have passed him by.

'Really?' I said, leaning forward in my seat. I recognised the feeling left over from my own policing days when I realised that someone I was in the midst of interviewing had just said something I could totally discredit. It was only because I was so upset that I didn't gloat from the realisation that I had actual evidence. I held my phone in front of me, screen towards the officer. 'Let me show you a video I recorded last week.'

I watched him peer at the flickering images. 'I'll help you out: that's our land, our private land, and you can see a dozen or so dogs running. They're running because this hunter behind the wheel of his Suzuki Vitara, who is not only trespassing on our land, is deliberately driving at the dogs. It's an open field with space all around. Not only has he no justification for being there, he has all the room he needs to drive away without driving at our dogs.'

I paused and stared at him. I tried so hard to stop myself flying into a rage, and besides, I needed to let the interpreter catch up with me. Our Bulgarian friend was respectful of authority figures, whereas I didn't care if the red mist enshrouded me. Never mind my policing days – when I had been a nurse, I had been very happy to deal with condescending consultants with their alarming attitudes when they were on their ward rounds. I was having none it then, and I was having none of it now. The dismissive policeman might not have spoken any English, but he got the idea. I stood with my hands on my hips and shouted at him, 'I'm clearly wasting my time.' I was so angry that they weren't going to take it any further.

I'll always stand up for what's right; I've always questioned and challenged things, and I've done that in every career I've had. It's not because I want to cause a problem but because I want to do the right thing. I probably got up the policeman's nose a little bit. Bulgaria is still quite a patriarchal society so a shouting, confrontational woman, especially a foreign one, is something the men find difficult to deal with. I found this debacle particularly hard to comprehend because I'd done everything right. I respect authority, and I'd done everything by the book, yet they still wouldn't investigate it. It was only at the point when I showed him the video that he took down the registration and said that he would look into it.

With reluctance, he produced a pen and a notebook and wrote down the registration number and then told me, 'That's about all I can do for you.'

Outside in the car park, the sun was beating down on us, vehicles meandered by, and people walked along the pavements as they went about their business. I couldn't help feeling as though this was it. We were finally beaten.

'Anthony, why are we putting ourselves through this?' I leant back against the bonnet of our car. 'It's time to go home.'

'I know,' he said, his expression matching my own battle-worn one.

'No. I mean home. Perhaps it's time to go back to England. What are we even doing here? They've poisoned our dogs. Benny No Neck was the most amazing, not to mention harmless, old boy. And Hugo was reserved for adoption, for crying out loud. We brought him back from the brink of death, nursed him to good health and he had a new home waiting for him with the best family.'

'Hey, come on,' he said as he walked around the pickup to join me. 'We'll work it out, we always do.'

Not for the first time, I was grateful that our marriage is as strong as it is and that we're in it together. This wasn't the first time that people had tried to bully us out of Bulgaria, and I doubted it would be the last. The hideous situation was compounded by my belief in the criminal justice system as a former police officer.

No one had ever warned me that rescuing dogs was going to be this hard.

31.

There's Good News and Bad News

Anthony – Then – July 2020

There were dark times ahead: the full realisation had hit us that there were people who hated us and the shelter so much, they would go to the extremes of threatening us and killing our dogs. Dogs we had taken from their streets. It made no sense to us at all. After Cleo went missing and Emma saw someone hiding in the bushes with a gun – outside of hunting season – we were wary. Wary but not about to walk away. Emma and I discussed moving back to England. Not only did we want to stay, we couldn't walk out on the dogs. Besides, the municipality had always had our backs. The people who mattered supported us, and we would have been powerless without them.

The Benny No Neck incident resulted in coverage on Bulgarian television. At the time, there were three main terrestrial TV channels, and the poisoning was included on a programme whereby Lucy was interviewed about Benny. Extreme animal cruelty still shocks, and the municipality is as passionate about stopping it as we are.

The team was growing, so there was greater strength in numbers too. Pauline Trent and her husband Andy, both originally from England, moved here in 2016 from their home in Turkey. They live in Zaya, a village close to ours, with its own street cat problems. They brought their dog and eight cats – all neutered – with them from Turkey and set about fundraising to neuter the local stray cats. As well as tackling this particular issue, over time they have raised money for Street Hearts and, if that weren't enough, Pauline gave up her time to carry out unpaid work for us here at the shelter.

Another positive to spur us on was the chance to make another application to Battersea Dogs and Cats Home, this time for a grant towards wages. For the first time, Pauline was going to get paid. Dan had filled out the grant application, which included funding for his own position. He detailed everything he did on a daily basis and a list of his responsibilities. It was an exciting moment when it was approved. All this time, Dan had worked here in exchange for his board and lodging. Finally, over a year later, he was actually going to get paid.

No sooner had we found out that the money was coming, Dan hit us with some news that we expected, yet dreaded. He had applied for a job in England and would be leaving in September. He had successfully applied for a role working for Cats Protection in Liverpool. The work centred on bringing about the neutering of both owned and feral cats – something that Emma and I were very proud of him for doing. The shelter was undoubtedly a better place for having Dan in it and we wouldn't be anywhere as successful as we are without him. We were going to miss him.

Just when we thought things might settle down and we could have some semblance of a normal summer, I received another call from the monastery. It sounded like the panicked voice of the same monk who had called about his errant peacock. This time I understood the word cat and that it was stuck in the bell tower. We obliged and drove over there.

By the time I pulled up in the pickup, the cat had managed to get itself into a tree adjacent to the bell tower. The only way I could fathom to get to the cat was to go into the bell tower, climb down the side of the bell tower to the bell tower wall, across the high, stone-flagged roof and try to coax the cat back off the tree. I climbed to the top of the bell tower and I was about to climb down when it struck me: *what am I thinking?* A bit like the peacock, if the cat got up there, it would probably have got back down again. As interesting as I found it in the bell tower, I decided against my initial plan.

As I scanned the skyline for peacocks – perhaps the cat had seen one on the roof's apex and tried to get itself a snack – I called our friend Catherine. She lived about ten minutes' drive from us, and more importantly, she was a climber.

I explained that there was a cat stuck up a tree in a monastery, and, like you do when friends make such a request – we've all been there – she said she would help and be with me in about ten minutes.

By the time Catherine arrived and joined me at the top of the bell tower, the monks had got bored and left us to it. Catherine climbed out of the bell tower and down the side onto the roof, across the roof and tried to catch the cat. While she was shouting at the cat, it walked away and walked down the trunk of the tree. Meanwhile, me and Catherine were left on the roof. Catherine shimmied away across the roof to the bell tower but, as agile as she was, she wasn't tall enough to pull herself back up. I had to squeeze past her on the roof and climb back up into the tower. Once inside, I couldn't reach down far enough to haul her back up, so left with no other choice, I went off in search of a ladder. Eventually I found a wooden ladder, not the sturdiest, but I tested it to make sure it would take my weight, so knew it would take Catherine's.

I carried it to the bell tower and started to climb the winding staircase. Ever climbed a nineteenth-century Bulgarian bell tower in a monastery? Ever tried to do it with a ladder? Don't, just don't. It took forever.

When I got to the top, I lowered the ladder out of the side of the tower onto the roof so that Catherine could reach it and climb back up. Then we had to pull the ladder back in and try to go back down the staircase with it. Getting the ladder back down seemed a lot worse than going up. I'd had enough by this time, so making sure that the monks, cats, peacocks and everything else was out of the way, I threw it out of the bell tower. It hit the ground, shattered into a thousand pieces and made the cat look round with the sort of disdain that only a cat can pull off.

Spoiler alert The monks stopped calling after that.

32

Dan's Story

Dan Gorman, volunteer

I can honestly say that, even if I live for another sixty years, being a part of Street Hearts is without a single doubt the best thing I will ever do. There were so many memorable moments. For the first year, it was only the three of us there permanently. We had some volunteers coming to the shelter for a week or two, but that was about the only assistance. How Emma and Anthony had managed to do the thankless work they undertook for two or three years, notwithstanding everything they have achieved since, I don't know. I admire them both so much for what they do. I think there are a very small number of people in the world who could persevere. The odds have always been stacked against them, yet still they achieve incredible result after incredible result.

The Bulgarian summer brings forty-degree temperatures; winter involves three feet of snow or mud – the pathways weren't gravelled when I was there, so we were wading through a bog in the worst of the rain. When it snowed heavily, sometimes we couldn't open the pen doors and we'd have to take a shovel to dig out the snow first. There were times the snow would be up to your knees. You had to plough through it to create paths to be able to walk through the shelter. On the pack walks, you'd end up with one long train of dogs and people, as everyone would just follow the path forged by whoever was in front – usually one of us. Even though it could be below zero, you quickly worked up a sweat doing this.

In the summer heat we'd often start work earlier in the morning because it would quickly become too hot for the dogs on the walks. It was tough work cleaning in that heat, but it still needed to be done, so you had to persevere.

The endless cleaning and looking after the dogs resulted in my T-shirts developing holes. Visitors to the shelter took pity on me and donated a bag of T-shirts for me to wear. One of them was adorned with 'Flat Cap and Whippet Day Pontefract 2019'. I wore it endlessly, even when we had a videographer arrive to film us. I think it was Anthony who said, 'Go and get that T-shirt off, you're not wearing that.' The top became a running joke, so I left it for my successor to wear after I'd gone. I'm not sure if she ever put it on.

When Emma asked if I wanted to live with them at Street Hearts, I hadn't known either of them for that long and over two reasonably short periods. We all got on very well, and I know that they wouldn't have asked me otherwise. I knew what an amazing opportunity it was to be a part of the team for twelve months; plus I would gain further invaluable experience working with animals.

It took about twelve months before Shandy and Sherry were truly comfortable around me. After that, I spent a lot more time with them; I felt a real connection with them. All of this took hours and hours over the course of twelve months. I'd start off in one corner of the kennel, they were in another and we would take it from there. They were so scared, yet over time they became a lot more confident. I have a lovely video of Shandy at one side of a field and me at the other, I called her and she ran towards me. It was brilliant. Shandy and Sherry were probably my two favourites, partly because of the time I spent with them. Shandy was adopted about a month after I left, and I've since been in touch with her adopter. It's amazing how much dogs can teach a person – I'll always remember those two.

Throughout my time at Street Hearts, I went on three or four transport trips back to the UK. My first was at the end of November 2019, where I said goodbye to Tilly, and it was great to see the dogs on their final journey. Most of the dogs in the van I had spent a considerable amount of time with and so it was emotional being able to hand the dogs to their new owners.

Emma and Anthony tried to make me cry – I didn't, by the way – but these transport runs were the closest I came. The dogs were coming from the worst moments of their lives; through illness, injury, neglect and abandonment to rehabilitation, training and socialisation. I had got to know them and this was the part where they had found families and they were on their final journey with Street Hearts. It was the last piece of the puzzle. Not many people ever get such an incredibly rewarding experience. The dogs were happy, the adopters were happy and I felt lucky to be a part of it. It's impossible to measure the impact we've had on not only the dogs, but the people. It wasn't always easy, and it was downright challenging at times. It was a lovely nineteen months of my life and I'll always cherish these memories.

The work I did with Street Hearts allowed me to get my job with Cats Protection. I facilitate the neutering of cats; sometimes the strays are brought in from the streets and other times I trap them, have them neutered and return them. I owe it to Emma and Anthony for giving me the chance to gain such incredible experience with the cats and dogs. As is the case in Bulgaria, throughout the United Kingdom there are many cat welfare issues. To stop animals suffering, we are helping to educate people about vaccinations for their cats, microchips and neutering, and we are a vital contact in the community.

One of the things that made working at Street Hearts so special was that the dogs are free-running with so much space. The pack walks are unique and the dogs seemed so content. The whole place had a positive energy, and I suppose that also stemmed from Emma and Anthony. Even though I left years ago, I took so much away with me and still wear my Street Hearts T-shirt.

Emma and Anthony are two of the nicest people. They are welcoming and supportive, and I've gone on to achieve my ambitions, largely down to them and their encouragement. Due to their welcoming and supportive personalities, I adjusted to being around them, something that takes time for me when I meet new people. I became a lot more confident in myself and they helped me to be a better person.

Other than the amazing experiences with animals, living a total adventure in the Bulgarian countryside with two of the nicest people, I rescued dogs and cats, drove a tractor, was turned into a coffee snob (I can't drink instant coffee anymore) and made memories I'll cherish for the rest of my life. I can't thank Emma and Anthony enough.

33.

Good Education

Emma – Then – September 2020

When we first arrived in Bulgaria and saw the dogs on the streets, our impression was that street dogs actually came from the streets: feral dogs that mated and produced unwanted puppies, so the circle continued. However, the problem is exacerbated by the daily occurrence here that dogs are dumped by owners and families who no longer want them. This is what has to change.

I used to see no reason at all why we needed to have children visit us at Street Hearts. I didn't think that the shelter was any place for them. But then we came to understand we had to break the pattern of behaviour, and to do this, we needed to educate people, starting with the younger generation. My focus now is on how many children we can bring to the shelter and educate.

We have so much passion to make this fundamental change in everyone's mindsets, both young and old, but starting with the children's shift in how they perceive animals. Hopefully, these kids who come and visit us and see the work we do and why we do it won't be dumping their own dogs on the streets when they no longer need them, can't care for them or can't be bothered with them.

Almost every time we're called out, we see the problem and that a lack of understanding and knowledge sits behind it. In September, Anthony and I were asked to go and help in a village called Yantra. We found four dogs and seven puppies in a horrific state in someone's yard. The owner told us that he was going to dump the females and the puppies, so we took them all away and set to work. We took the adult females (one we named Connie) to the vet to be neutered, ensured they all had a few baths, enough food and received the medical treatment they needed. At the time, one of the puppies we named Mr Wiggles due to a severe worm infestation. He also had mange and a worrying weight of less than one kilogram. We doubted that he would survive, and such was the severity of the worm infestation and overall neglect, he was probably a day or two from death when we got to him.

Not only did he get his happy ever after, but his terrible condition also gave him the best name ever. When he was adopted weeks after his recovery, Rachel Harrison, his adopter, promised that she wouldn't change his name.

Our education programme includes a lesson plan for schools, covering vet care and the correct food for a dog. Dogs are often fed bread in Bulgaria, something that prevents them from developing and growing properly, leading to all kinds of health issues further down the line. One man who asked for our help with his dogs had no idea that the four bags of bread he bought daily for them was more expensive than giving them kibble. A ten-kilogram bag of kibble here costs 13 leva/€6.50 and would last a week. The bread cost 19.60 leva, which is just short of €10.

One day we'd love to have visitors coming here on a Sunday and taking some of the dogs out for a walk. We have some stunning scenery and it would really help people connect with dogs and help socialise the dogs with new people. All of this takes time though, a resource we never have enough of. If we could stretch the budget or get funding, it would be incredible to have a volunteer co-ordinator. Ideally, two more members of staff would help.

One of the many things I learnt from Battersea was that we have to treat the shelter like a business. Our first few years were far from ideal, yet we've realised that we have to be flexible, and a fluid approach is the only way to cope. I wished we had learnt quicker. I value the importance of dog training, rather than letting them get on with it. Everyone has new ideas, including our volunteers. I'm always excited when they come along and suggest something we haven't tried, or a way of how we can improve on something.

Some of the volunteers have impressed us so much that we've offered them jobs. After we got the shelter manager grant from Battersea – applied for by Dan Gorman – we were able to offer Stefi, a German woman who was initially here for a brief time, a full-time job.

This was the year we applied for a project development manager grant and got that too. Without it, we wouldn't have been able to do any of the outreach work that has been so vital in saving hundreds of dogs. It has helped towards the education programme and the running costs of our previous Land Rover, enabling us to get out into the countryside and capture dogs and their litters from rubbish tips, beneath bridges and from derelict buildings.

Rachel Harrison, adopted Mr Wiggles and Connie

I've known Emma for decades. We grew up in the same village, and since Emma and Anthony established their shelter, I've followed them on social media, marvelling at how they were managing to do so much in Bulgaria to help the street dogs. Prior to adopting our dogs from Street Hearts, my husband and I had a Jack Russell called Hovis who, when he died, left us both utterly devastated. When we felt we were ready to have another dog in our lives, we said that we would only do it if we adopted. Contacting Emma seemed the obvious and natural thing to do.

I told Emma that I wanted a female; she warned me that the dogs they had were often larger dogs, not Jack Russell-size. Then I saw one of their litters of puppies they rescued from a village, along with the mum Connie. I instantly fell for Connie, but Emma told me that there was a very good chance that, due to how frightened and timid she was, she would live out her days with them at Street Hearts.

We wanted to adopt Mr Waffles, one of Connie's pups, and briefly considered getting both Mr Waffles and Mr Wiggles until we concluded that two puppies would probably be too much. We decided that Mr Wiggles was the one for us.

In December 2020, our puppy came over with Anthony and Emma and, along with the rest of the transport run, had to be kept in quarantine for two days before he could be collected. In that time, I came down with Covid, so my sister-in-law went and picked him up. She has never been a dog person, and never wanted a dog, but Mr Wiggles seemed to change that. She said to me, 'I'm asking Emma for a dog.' It wasn't long before she adopted Joseph from them.

Mr Wiggles was so quiet when we got him home. It was a little bit strange seeing a puppy so still. That all changed within seven days: a week later, he was dragging everything out onto the floor, chewing towels and behaving exactly as you would expect a puppy to behave. We started to take him on holiday with us, to Wales, to Scotland and different parts of England. He loved it and we couldn't be happier.

About a year after we adopted Mr Wiggles, Emma contacted me and asked how I felt about adopting Connie. She knew that I had always liked her, and life in the shelter was no longer working out for her. Street Hearts had spent a lot of time working with her to improve her confidence, but as often happens with sanctuary dogs, the shelter environment became too much for her. As her behaviour had started to regress, a new home somewhere else was becoming the best option for Connie.

To prepare Mr Wiggles for who was about to come and live with us, we showed him video footage on the television of Connie, sent to us from Street Hearts. We said, 'This is your mummy. Remember her?' Despite what people may say about dogs not realising what they are looking at on video, I would say that he recognised her.

Emma brought Connie over to England and we agreed that it was best to meet on neutral territory. We met in a dog field, and

Mr Wiggles instantly knew Connie was his mum. Connie, on the other hand, looked a bit shell-shocked. For the first few days, she seemed traumatised and I think it took her a couple of weeks to realise who Mr Wiggles was. It was six weeks before she realised that she was here to stay.

Connie has always been a terrible passenger in a car; she gets very travel sick. Once she had been here for a reasonable period of adjustment, we took the dogs to a caravan for a holiday. When we came home, she behaved like a different dog. It was as if she realised that she was with us permanently and this was always going to be her home. No matter what happened, no matter where we took her, she understood that she would always come back and be with us.

Connie didn't bark, play with toys or warm to visitors when she first arrived. Although she still doesn't play much and is shy of strangers in the home, she has improved around people. She will also yap at me to tell me that it's time to go out. She likes to steal my socks and lick them. There is never any chewing, just soggy socks.

Street Hearts lead train the dogs while they are in the shelter. Our fabulous dog walker also works with Mr Wiggles on the lead, building on everything he has already been shown. As my husband and I work full-time, we have an excellent dog walker or use doggy day care. Mr Wiggles is very protective of his mum: if she is at the groomer's, Mr Wiggles is beside himself that she isn't at home.

Connie is still jumpy and on edge around loud noises when she is out on a walk, such as the sound of lorries hurtling past. Again, she has improved over the time she has been with us, and no doubt, will get even better still, but it's something we are aware of.

We take them to dog parks, and they are allowed to run freely in the allotments in our village. They love to come along with me when I'm planting and sowing. I have to keep an eye on anything they think they are at liberty to dig up. When you have a dog – or dogs – you accept that sometimes, your cabbages will end up dug up long before they should be.

Mr Wiggles is a large black dog with a white chest, and Connie looks like a small fat spaniel. I sent off Mr Wiggles's DNA and it came back with a mixture of nineteen different breeds, some of which I hadn't even heard of. He's a combination of Russian balaka, chow chow, Gordon setter, Bulgarian sheepdog, Portuguese Podengo, Yorkshire terrier, miniature dachshund and chihuahua, amongst others! I hope to get Connie's DNA sent off soon.

It was from this that I managed to find out where his brother Mr Waffles was. In 2022, we met up with his sibling and his adopters in Wales. The dogs had so much fun.

Connie has certainly made herself at home over the time she has been with us. She learnt that she can headbutt the spare bedroom door open at night, leaving her easy access to the spare bed. Connie and Mr Wiggles then climb onto the bed and cuddle up for the night. Although they are both equally guilty, she is definitely the culprit. The noise of the door being banged open in the night is a giveaway.

We have tried to do what we can to support Anthony and Emma and the Street Hearts team. We got into a conversation about dogs with the manager of our local DFS store when we were looking for a new sofa. She has an overseas rescue dog, so we chatted about our experience and how much we love Connie and Mr Wiggles. She offered to supply Street Hearts with any spare sofa cushions the store couldn't use or resell. I called Emma and they were delighted to take as many as DFS could supply. Most dog beds aren't as flame retardant as sofa cushions because of the necessary health and safety regulations around soft furnishings. They not only make brilliant dogs' beds, but it also means that they don't end up in landfill. I know that Emma and Anthony can put them to good use.

The education centre they have established, welcoming children to visit the shelter and learn about the dogs, as well as visits into schools, is another step in the right direction. Street Hearts' success has meant that other municipalities call on them to help out in other villages. Emma and Anthony never turn an animal away. The shelter is a refuge to dogs, cats, horses, pigs and chickens. I think if an elephant turned up in the village, they would give it a home.

34.

Renée the Rescue Bus

Anthony – Then – October 2020

The year had been turbulent, and yet there were so many posi-
tives to look back on. The education programme was taking
shape, and every transport run we completed was another
achievement for the twenty dogs on board. We always try to
move forward and look at the fantastic people we have met and
who have helped us along the way. Miroslav Semov, when he was
elected Dryanovo's mayor, did so much for us and the street
dogs. His successor, Trifon Panchev, and the deputy mayor of
Tryavna, Marin Marinov, have made such a positive difference
too. They want to see an end to abandoned dogs on the streets,
and we know that we wouldn't get very far without these people
and their unwavering support. As time went on, there was an
increase in locals who approached us to have their dogs neutered
by Dimitar, our much-trusted vet, so Emma and I knew that the
message was slowly and surely getting through. Along with Trifon
and Marin backing Street Hearts, it was this trickling through of
positivity and the support of well-wishers at home and via social

media that kept us going. Without the very same supporters adopting our dogs – or in fact any rescue dog from any country – all the money and resources in the world wouldn't mean anything without people opening their homes to a former street dog.

Of course, it was these same supporters who answered our request to donate again for the second bus that we needed as backup for Frankie the Furever Bus. In October, I drove our second bus, largely funded by our incredible supporters, on its inaugural transport run to the UK. We named the second bus Renée the Rescue Bus in honour of the starving hunting dog I picked up by the roadside in Gostilitsa. Not only did Renée make a full recovery, but eighteen months later, she was heading for a wonderful new life in Stockport with her adopter Nicki Irvine. Nicki has been a long-time follower and supporter of Dogs 4 Rescue, which is how she came to hear about Street Hearts.

Nicki Irvine's story

I adopted my dog Branston in 2019 when he was about five months old – I still have two of his baby teeth. Street Hearts had been trying to catch Sara, Branston's mum, for years. Sara was roaming around Dryanovo, almost permanently pregnant with one litter or another, but they simply couldn't catch her. At last they managed to get her with her final litter of puppies. Most of them subsequently travelled across with Anthony and Emma to Dogs 4 Rescue, where they were rehomed. That's how I came to adopt Branston. He was very good in the house and was generally well behaved. Due to lockdown I had been working from home most of the time, and that was continuing, which was part of my reason for getting a second dog.

Prior to Branston, I had a Staffie cross ridgeback, a rescue from the RSPCA. I was used to one dog, but two was slightly different. The deciding factor was when I read Renée's story. I saw on social media that Anthony had picked up her malnourished, skinny body from beside the road and put her in the back of his truck. It took about eighteen months for her to be nursed back to health and anywhere ready for a new home. She arrived at Dogs 4 Rescue one Saturday night so, the following morning, I drove over to pick her up and bring her back here. I took Branston along to make sure there wasn't going to be any problems between the two of them.

I walked Renée up and down the lane beside Dogs 4 Rescue and marvelled at how trusting she was. I had seen the pictures of her online when Anthony was carrying her and read that another five were chained up with no food or water, one having starved to death. It was hard to believe that this was the same dog. I saw her little face and knew what a special dog she was, although it didn't stop me worrying that she might start fighting with Branston. Anthony and Emma said goodbye to her and placed her in my boot next to him.

The pair of them were no trouble at all on the journey home. We all went out in the garden when we got back and then the dogs had a play together. At first, she seemed a little wary of her new surroundings; she was sick on one of the rugs and tried to hide it, as if she was worried that she would get into trouble. Things improved when she started to relax and settled into a chair, looking like she had a big smile on her face.

It took time for her to completely settle in. She would growl at the television, leading me to think she had never seen one. She has the most beautiful temperament, but even so, she didn't like Branston coming anywhere near her when she was asleep. I'm not sure if she had been used to sleeping in a barn with other dogs, but for the first year after she arrived, she would jump up and run at Branston if he disturbed her when she was asleep. Poor Branston was in trouble a lot to begin with.

Even though Branston is bigger than Renée, she is most definitely the boss. Branston's background means that he was used to hiding away and he's nervous of men, while Renée is the opposite. When we're out on a walk, she will stop in front of people so they can stroke her. What's happened as a result of her outgoing personality is that Branston's confidence has grown. That's such a great thing to watch happen. They both have their quirks: Branston likes to alert me to cars parking outside our house, while Renée prefers to bark at dogs being walked along our street. She's great with other dogs and doesn't make a sound when we encounter them on a walk, whether it be in a park or along the canal towpaths. It's just her way of letting me know they are there.

Renée acts like a little old lady at times: she'll jump up onto the sofa and won't move, even if Branston climbs up next to her. She loves it when Branston nibbles on her ears, and it makes for great entertainment for my son and me. The first time the two dogs cuddled up together was magical. They each have their own spots they prefer to curl up in, as well as where they like to sleep at night. Renée sleeps in my son's room and Branston sleeps in mine. When it's time to go to bed, we all go up the stairs and the dogs wait outside their respective bedroom doors.

The pair of them know my routine and can tell when it's the weekend. On the days when I'm working, they don't even bother to come downstairs until 10 a.m., yet on Saturdays and Sundays, they know it's cuddle time and make an earlier appearance. We're so lucky to have these two; they are fabulous dogs.

Because Renée is an ex-hunting dog, I can't let her off the lead when I take her out for her regular walks. The only time I can let her run completely free is when I book a secure field. The two of them can chase around, Renée easily outrunning Branston. Neither of them has any insecurities when it comes to meeting other dogs. Their background means that they are friendly with the other dogs we meet and, thanks to Emma and Anthony's ethos of not kennelling the dogs individually and the work they put in with the lead training, they are so extremely well behaved. They don't come with lots of problems, so whenever I get into a conversation with anyone about where they came from, they are usually astonished to hear that they were street dogs. People find it difficult to believe how calm they are on a lead, but it spreads such a positive message about Street Hearts and, of course, Dogs 4 Rescue. Their training and the caring environment they find at both rescue shelters makes them well-adjusted dogs, ideal for a family home. I know that there is negativity out there relating to foreign dogs in the UK, but I have to say that I have never come across it.

One of my neighbours has a dog called Timmy, a former Street Hearts' rescue. I think that he was at the shelter just after Branston left and must have known Renée when she was there.

She always does the dance of joy whenever we see Timmy. My village has a total of five former Street Hearts' dogs, along with rescues from Romania and Cyprus. It's quite the community here. I collect towels, blankets and other supplies. Laura Norrey works for Street Hearts and her parents pick everything up and she stores the goods until Anthony is over with the next transport run. He then runs it back to the shelter.

I have nothing but praise for what Emma and Anthony do, they are just amazing. Even in the event of something not working out, they are quick to put it right. Street Hearts always keeps in touch and helps with any backup adopters might need. The support is fantastic. In March 2023, Anthony dropped in to see us when he was on his way back to Bulgaria. As soon as Renée realised who he was, she cuddled up next to him on the sofa. That was something really special to see.

35.

The Mayor of Dryanovo

Trifon Panchev

For our town to have Anthony and Emma is a godsend. They fund the building costs of their shelter, as well as energy costs, food, water, maintenance and the ongoing vet bills. Of course, the municipality helps with whatever we can, but even so, we can't solve all of the problems with money alone. A lot of it is about the mentality of the Bulgarian people, and how we educate the younger generation is important. We have to show them that animals are not the enemy and to encourage other attitudes away from the brutality and bad practices that happen here every day.

There are a number of Bulgarian municipalities with more money available to them than ours has, and from that overall budget comes the cost of a municipality-run dog shelter. One of the biggest concerns about a municipality shelter, once again, comes down to people's attitudes towards dogs. If there's a problem with the dog, it's off to the shelter, whereas they might have only got one in the first place because they felt obligated to. If they feel compelled to get one, they probably won't appreciate it and as a result of their poor decision-making, this is transferred to the unwanted dog and it's surrendered to an already overwhelmed dog shelter. So, the problem goes on.

The culture in the many small villages dotted around the mountains and countryside is one of the fundamental reasons why we're in the scenario we have today. Many of the men are hunters – of boar and deer – so dogs are a part of their hunting way of life. The hounds are used from the first stages of their lives like instruments until, that is, they are of no further use. There's no retirement for these working animals, they're merely thrown out onto the street. They aren't thought of as living creatures when their usefulness has expired, and this is the mentality that has to change through targeting people with educational information and campaigns on how to look after animals.

If I tell someone that they should get their dog castrated, their reply to me is 'why don't you castrate your kids?'. It's a bygone era attitude, with no law to obligate them to do so. If a dog were to attack and kill someone, the government would soon enough intervene and make sure that the owner was suitably punished, yet nothing is ever enforced for failure to register a dog. If the threat of avoiding this requirement were to be a custodial sentence, this would be a good thing and would stop the problem.

Dryanovo has something like a thousand dogs and only 10 per cent of them are registered. The municipality simply doesn't have the capacity to ask their citizens to do it. If the government changed the laws to make non-compliance more stringently punishable and gave us another 300 police officers to do it, that may bring it to a close. Realistically, that isn't going to happen. Bulgarian municipalities are the world's most obligated organisations. Research has shown that mayors of municipalities have 5,000 different laws and regulations to work with, so the street dogs are just one thing on a very lengthy agenda. Rather than relying on the municipality or the police, perhaps a totally separate entity should take on the task.

I was already working in the municipality prior to being voted in as mayor, so I've always tried to view the situation from a separate standpoint and make meaningful changes where I can. I was born in Sofia, but I knew this area, as both my mother and grandfather live in Dryanovo and I have friends in the district too. I was a lawyer in Sofia and have a background in an agricultural business breeding sheep. I fail to recall a time that my family didn't own dogs, and as my grandparents lived in a village, the way of life was to have animals. Even now I have two dogs. I used to have two pitbulls, but sadly only one now. Our other dog is a female husky Canadian wolf cross so I know the value of family pets and how to look after them.

Anthony and Emma were already operating the shelter when I became mayor in November 2019. What was becoming another complication was the street dogs from Tryavna being dumped here or ending up in Dryanovo anyway. The situation was a difficult one, yet Anthony and Emma both worked as tirelessly and with the same motivation and enthusiasm in Tryavna as they have here in Dryanovo.

We're dealing with ingrained beliefs and what went on historically in socialist times. The street dog problem was easily dealt with by shooting them, which the vast majority accepted as the norm. If the animals aren't there, they aren't a problem. It's not the dogs that are the issue, it's the people who put them there. Every single day someone else chucks his dog out onto the streets. The situation is further perpetuated by Bulgarians believing that their dogs should be aggressive canine security guards. Twenty years ago, every house in every village had a chained dog in the front yard. There was terrible amounts of crime and the rationale for keeping a dog in those conditions was that it would bark if anyone entered the property and possibly bite any intruders. There is less crime today, partly due to a transient population with many leaving for winter and returning in summer. Fewer people around leads to less criminal activity.

I don't believe it's possible to resolve all of these issues without changing the law. We need changes in the current legislation. Our shelter isn't municipality owned, still Anthony and Emma have to adhere to the rules and regulations in order to continue to operate. Someday, the entire sorry situation will be better, but we have to be patient. It's going to take decades.

36.

If Pigs Could Fly

Anthony – Then – February 2021

Bus write-offs, swine flu and then Covid stopped us from doing many things, but it couldn't dampen our enthusiasm for rescuing animals. And by animals, we were – and still are – in the non-profitable business of saving dogs, not pigs, some cats too, but not pigs. You'll be familiar by now with my seismic shift from farmer to vegetarian, so when Emma asked me if we could take in two tiny pigs, my answer was an unreserved yes.

Some years ago, an English woman who lived in Bulgaria had adopted a dog from us. This was not long after we started to take dogs in, around the time that we were adamant that we weren't going to open a shelter, but nevertheless did exactly that. When Emma had dropped the dog off, she carried out a home check, met the woman's two other dogs and noticed that she also had two tiny pot-bellied pigs.

Tragically, several years later, this poor woman was murdered by a Bulgarian man. With no one else to look after the dog following her death, we were asked if we could take our former

Street Hearts dog back, as well as the two other dogs. Emma agreed and was then asked if she would take the little pigs. Emma regaled me with tales of the tiny pigs she had seen snuffling and snorting around the woman's property. I said, 'OK, let's take the pigs as well.' If Emma wanted them, I wasn't going to argue.

Someone dropped the three homeless dogs at the shelter (they were all later adopted) and, for the first time in months, Emma and I were able to get away for a couple of rare days off. We threw some stuff into a bag and drove away in the pickup, pleased that we had at last managed to get away from it all. On our way back home, chilled and relaxed, we thought that it would be a good idea to pick the pigs up before someone decided to eat them. The thought of local villagers making entrées out of these two cuties was too much, so we detoured on our way home to get them. We were still dressed smartly from our couple of days away, our usual Street Hearts uniform hanging up at home.

When we got to the house, it was still a murder crime scene and full of police officers. As we pulled up in the pickup, we parked close to the canal ditch that ran outside the house. A quick glance at the ditch revealed used disposable gloves that police and forensic officers had presumably worn, alongside a number of forensic swabs. We looked down at the misshapen gloves, many inside out where they had been clumsily removed from hands, and then back up at each other, before turning our gaze towards the crime scene.

'This is bizarre,' said Emma. 'It's still a crime scene. Whatever you do, don't touch anything and don't leave your fingerprints anywhere.'

As I was about to add, 'You don't have to tell me twice,' the mayor of the local area arrived to take care of the paperwork. Moving pigs carries a disease risk, which means it can only be done with a licence or written agreement. After we exchanged pleasantries and told the mayor that we had been asked to rescue the pigs, he looked us up and down, dressed in our best going-away attire, glared at our pickup and said, 'How exactly are you going to move these pigs?'

I said, 'They're only small, we'll pick them up and put them in the back of the truck.'

The mayor said, 'You what? They're at least 120 kg each.'

I looked at Emma and said, 'You told me that they were the size of Little Blackie! Hold one in each hand, you said. Are you insane?' From the look on Emma's face, she could see the anger sweep across mine. Being an ex-farmer, I'm used to pigs, used to the size they are and how unwieldy they are. They aren't particularly interested in being picked up – because they're pigs. Pigs don't like that kind of thing. Possibly I was overreacting, but I was also being realistic about the prospect of the next stage in this incredulous scenario.

The mayor, with a smirk on his face, wrote out the document for us to sign. There were about four or five expats there who had known the murdered woman. They had been taking it in turns to feed the pigs who turned out to be named Ziggy and Gizmo.

We entered the murder scene and that was when it really got interesting. There were two humongous pigs running around the garden with an entourage of expats all shouting 'Ziggy! Gizmo!' All they were interested in was the bag of fresh vegetables that people were scattering all over the ground. The pigs' home was a large shed at the rear of the garden and the assembled crowd were trying to entice them back inside it with food. I looked at Emma and wondered how on earth we were going to get two enormous pigs into the back of our pickup truck. The back is about three feet off the ground and jumping pigs are about as rare as flying ones.

I scanned the garden for something useful and saw a big empty dog crate. I thought that the best idea would be to get the pigs inside it, one at time. By now, there were about six of us, including the vegetable throwing expats. If the plan went well, we could pick up the crate with a pig inside it and carry it to the truck. First we needed to get the pigs inside the shed, so we could shut them in, get the crate and then coax each of them inside it with some vegetables.

Once Ziggy was in the crate, I slammed the door shut. Dog crates aren't designed for pigs, but needs must. I couldn't get the pickup anywhere near to the shed because there were large mounds of sand all over the garden. The only option was for several of us to pick up the crate with Ziggy inside and carry it back through the crime scene and out of the main gate. With a bit of bowing and giving, the crate just about stood up to its task. One down, one to go.

We went back for Gizmo who was slightly less happy about going into the crate than Ziggy. I would describe his mood as irritable. We repeated the process: put the cage down, put some food down and waited for him to get inside. He wasn't really interested. We had to corner the pig and manipulate the crate backwards, so it was over the pig. The idea was to get Gizmo to slowly enter the crate. He wasn't convinced it was in his interests and took to banging about in his shed – possibly a pig's way of telling us to clear off. The crate was wobbling, creaking and cracking. It was far from perfect, but the best option we had. No one else in the pantomime production had ever touched a pig before, so other than throwing carrots at it, I had limited help.

Eventually we managed to pick up the crate and carry it through the garden gate to the pickup. As we got outside the gate, the pig went mental and trashed the cage. The cage fell apart, the pig jumped down and just bolted. [Note to all interested in the potential of pig rescue: pigs can jump down short distances, not necessarily up.] We were in a village, surrounded by forest and no obstacles to prevent an escape. The pig could have run as far as Paris, there was nothing to stop it.

Now we were faced with running around the village to catch Gizmo. What was abundantly clear was that shouting 'Gizmo' and lobbing carrots after it wasn't very effective, but it didn't stop the entourage. The pig was petrified. It was out of the garden it had known for the last three years, it was running around a village and to top it all, it had lost its friend which was in the truck slowly munching on a carrot that someone had left for it.

I found a pair of overalls in the back of the truck, put them on and chased after the pig. I tried to corner it, get it into various gardens, behind sheds, beside cars, wherever I could. I tried to coax it back to the garden, as that was the only secure place we had for it. This went on for two hours. It started to get dark. Meanwhile, the pig appreciation society was still shouting 'Gizmo'. One by one, they got bored and drifted off until there were only three left.

Eventually Gizmo was so worn out, it stood stock still on a grass verge. All I had in the truck was a dog's slip lead. A pig's neck is bigger than its head, especially true with the size of these two porkers. I wasn't sure exactly how this was going to work but it was all I had. I went for it; I lassoed the pig and it went bonkers. It started to drag back, charge at me, drag back and charge at me. With its tusks – oh, did I mention they both had enormous tusks? – it ripped my overalls all along the thigh. Fortunately, my leg was unscathed. I shouted at the expats to get the dog cage, as I had hold of the squealing pig by the dog slip lead, barely managing to hold on to him. I sent Emma to the truck to grab the cable ties from the back.

'Who carries cable ties?' said Emma over her shoulder as she ran towards the pickup.

'Luckily I do. Get them now,' I shouted as I held onto the manic pig with both hands.

The others brought the cage over to where I had hold of the screaming pig while Emma handed out the cable ties. I shouted over Gizmo's shrieks for everyone to cable-tie the cage back together. The pig was still putting up a fight, but I could see that he was getting more and more tired. The amateur pig-wranglers put the cage in front of the pig and I fed the lead through the cage as far as I could. I held on to the lead and we eased the cage back over the pig. It was exhausted by this time, so it had calmed down. This debacle might sound cruel, but the alternative was the pig being shot and eaten.

Emma went to get the truck and brought it as close as she could to the cage. The plan was to lift it into the truck. We hoisted up the creaking cage, but, of course, there was already a lose pig in the back. We opened the door gingerly, popped the second pig in the cable-tied cage beside it and shut the doors. I wasn't best pleased with all of this, as you can imagine. By now, it was just me and Emma in the village. It was pitch black.

'What are we going to do with them when we get home?' said Emma. 'I thought that we were going to put them in the clinic, but that's not going to happen, not now.'

We drove home and it was absolutely silent. Not a squeak from our passengers.

Once we got to the shelter, I still didn't know what we were going to do with them. I couldn't simply open the door. The back of the truck was too high and they were too fat to jump down. That would surely end with them breaking their legs. It was 9.30 p.m., dark, the rain was coming down in stair rods and I didn't have a clue what to do.

After I crashed Frieda, which was part dog transporter and part camper van, I put her wreckage 100 m or so from the house, in a clearing overlooking the valley. An Austrian lad who had previously stayed with us had moved into it and built a balcony in front of the van. I thought that the best option was for me to reverse the truck up to the balcony as it was about the same height as the truck. I would then drop the tailgate and get the pigs into the van and then shut the van door. It wasn't the best plan, but with nowhere else secure to put them, it had to work.

There were several flaws in the plan. Firstly, the bed was still inside the van. Secondly, the balcony didn't have any wire or panelling around it so it was open. Thirdly, there was a tree close to the spot where I needed to park. I started by cutting branches off the tree to make enough room before I could reverse the truck up. Finally, we emptied the van. Even that took ages: it was still raining, and everything had to be carried to a shed across to the other side of the house.

At the time, we were still in the process of building dog pens, so we got a couple of the full-size metal panels for the fences and put them around the balcony to stop the pigs from escaping. When everything was in place, I looked at Emma to make sure she was poised. I dropped the tailgate, opened the crate and luckily, the first pig trotted out and headed for the balcony. It walked into the van and the second one followed. I shut the van door behind them, leaned against it for a moment and breathed a sigh of relief. 'It's done,' I said. 'We've got them secured.'

'It's a good thing we've done there,' said Emma. I don't think that she could see how displeased I was in the faint light of the midnight hour.

'What are we going to do with two pigs, Emma?' I said through gritted teeth.

'Lead train them?' She gave a small laugh and when I failed to join in, said, 'Sorry, is it too soon?'

'We'll have to build a pen around the van, enclose the balcony and build a ramp so the pigs can get in and out.' I always have industrial ramps at the shelter so that I can easily drive the digger onto the trailer.

'Great idea,' said Emma. 'Perhaps in the morning when it's light and not raining?'

Emma had made enough helpful suggestions for one day, but she did have a point.

It took four days for me to build the ramp and pig pen. It was something I could have done without, and undoubtedly the pigs weren't too impressed with being shut inside a crashed bus for four days. They were frustrated and chewed everything inside it. When the pen was finished, I thought that the pigs could live in the van but would get used to walking up and down the ramp.

Pleased with my pig pen impro, I opened the van door to let them out. They even had a properly screened balcony in their new abode. Ziggy and Gizmo happily wandered down the ramp and snuffled around. But would they go back up it? No, of course not. That left them with nowhere to sleep and they were completely open to the elements. Emma made *ah* noises when I told her that they wouldn't use the ramp, so, naturally, I set about building them another shed inside the pen. That took another day. Because they couldn't live in one small pen, I had to fence about an acre of land within the forest so they had more open space. Pigs can live in small pens – it happens in the agricultural world – but there was no way we wanted that for them, even if I didn't want the poxy pigs in the first place. Now they were here, they were going to be well looked after. That took another two days to build the fence with leftover materials we had from one of the dog runs.

'Do you know what'll go well with the pigs?' said Emma when she came out to admire my handiwork. I knew what was coming. 'Chickens, you know I want chickens. I've wanted them since we came out here.'

'Oh, for— I'm going to make a coffee.' Five days, five long days that took me.

37.

Girl With No Name

Emma – Then – May 2021

Anthony didn't stay mad at me for long. As I tell people, we rarely fall out – although that's usually the point where he chips in with 'Yes, we do.' Besides, he knew how completely devastated I was over the loss of our venerable Roshy, who had passed away the previous month. We were both cut up about it, but I really loved that great bear of a dog. Wonderful Roshy had helped feral Bonnie to get over her fears, and then she became his wife. The two of them were inseparable. Bonnie was clearly heartbroken too. I didn't think that she would ever be the same again. Even though Roshy died of old age more than anything else, it still didn't stop me crying my eyes out when he passed away.

I didn't allow myself the luxury of wallowing in misery. We were busier than ever, and I had to get things ready for a new volunteer, Lauren Hoodless, who was arriving soon for a six-week stay. I hoped that was going to work out. I found myself hurrying back to the staff kitchen between our house and the dog runs. I passed by our oversized chicken run, our two rescue pigs scratch-

231

ing around in the dirt beside the clucking hens. The chickens didn't fit our mission statement either, but like Ziggy and Gizmo, my girls were all rescued animals. Their owner had died and Anthony and I were called to rescue their dogs, Scamp and Fred. I thought if we left the chickens behind, they would get eaten by the jackals. We were put through our paces that day too: one of the dogs was quite savage and tried to kill us – all in a day's work. Meanwhile, the deputy mayor who accompanied us owned a chain of vegetable shops which came in very handy when we needed some boxes to put the chickens in. He nipped off to one of his shops, got some boxes and presented us with our new chicken transport. Once the dog had stopped trying to rip our throats out, we took both dogs and the chickens back to the shelter. Anthony was delighted that, at last, someone was able to enjoy the modifications he had made to the crashed van. 'Picture the girls running up and down the ramp,' I said to him, my arms laden with chickens peeking out of their boxes. 'They'll have a bird's-eye view from that balcony.' He laughed and laughed. Well, no, he didn't. Nevertheless, he still helped me to put them in an empty dog pen until he had a chance to chicken-proof the fence. It might have been secure for pigs but not for chickens. He hardly complained once about the extra work.

I took a moment to watch the chickens pecking around on the ground between the pigs' trotters, some heading indoors towards the rusting shell of our old transport bus, given a new lease of life as a giant chicken coop.

I was under some time pressure by this stage to get what I needed from the staff kitchen, mostly cat food, which is excellent for feeding to petrified, hungry street dogs. Lucy, our

Bulgarian team member, had been contacted by a friend of a friend about a chained-up, heavily pregnant dog about half an hour's drive from the shelter. I needed to grab some more pouches of cat food before we set off. No matter the urgency, I took one more moment to think about Roshy, that absolute legend of a dog.

He's buried between the front field and the pig run, and never has a dog taught me so much. I was hopeful that whatever today's alert was about to bring, it would end with a dog having many incredible years to come, just like Roshy's happy ever after.

Lucy and I pulled up outside a single-storey concrete build-ing. It was a typical Bulgarian home, although according to Lucy's contact, it had been empty for some time after the occu-pant died. The neighbours who came out to speak to us confirmed that was the case and that the dog was behind the house. We often get interested parties who want to see what we are doing, mostly these days out of curiosity rather than the animosity we used to face. We weren't wasting time talking now we were here. Lucy and I walked along the side of the property, the house on one side and a ramshackle lean-to shelter to the other side. It was a corrugated iron roof held up by rope against poles pushed into the earth, making do as an open-sided shed for old planks of wood, mismatched tyres and general parapher-nalia. It wasn't the most secure, yet it was better than the sight that greeted us to the rear of the collection of backyard clutter.

I followed Lucy across the mud, careful not to lose my foot-ing. There was a wooden kennel around three feet by four, the base starting to rot away in the damp earth. I could see a dog's snout poking through the doorway, a chain disappearing somewhere inside. One end of it was attached to a bolt secured into the ground. A couple of slices of bread thrown down beside the kennel and an empty bucket gave some indication that someone had made an attempt to help this animal.

Once we coaxed this petrified girl out of the kennel, I could see that the chain was less than a metre long. This was how she had spent her life. She was a sweet girl and around thirteen years old, the size of a German shepherd. As she stood in front of me, I could tell that something was very wrong with her. She was initially defensive, so to minimise any risk to her or to us, we called our vet. He attended and sedated her so that we could move her to our clinic at Street Hearts with as little stress to her as possible. Even though she had had a harrowing life and had suffered from neglect, she still wagged her tail as I held out chunks of food, eating it gently from my palm.

With her safely loaded into the truck, I had a look inside her kennel. Unsurprisingly there was no bedding, or what bedding may once have been was decomposed, leaving a mess of threads and fibres resembling rotten fishing nets. The only other thing present inside her 'home' was filth. No one had cleaned up after this dog in a long while. It was time for our vet Dimitar to take a proper look at her so we knew what we were dealing with.

This Girl With No Name wasn't pregnant after all. She was riddled with tumours in her abdomen and had at least two litres of fluid around her organs from liver failure. The kindest thing that we could do for her was to let her pass away with dignity and free from pain. She deserved so much better.

I walked away from the clinic, sad that a dog had been, once again, left in such squalid conditions. As I crossed the courtyard,

I was cheered by the sight around me of the rescued dogs we had here in the shelter, some running and playing, the seniors lying and snoozing. At least these ones were safe, many waiting for kind-hearted folk to adopt them into their families.

As I had done every day since he passed away, I walked towards Roshy the Wonder Dog's final resting place. He completely stole my heart and I didn't want to let him go. He was an absolute superstar.

Roshy, I would have loved you to have met and been a big brother to the Girl With No Name. You would have been the absolute making of her. Rest in peace, my lovely boy.

38

How Bad Can It Get?

Lauren Hoodless, shelter manager

Working at Street Hearts was my first immersive volunteer animal experience – and what an experience it's been. I came out here in June 2021 for a six-week period and never looked back. I'm from Wilmslow, Cheshire, and graduated from university with a degree in commercial hair and make-up. My life changed when I adopted a rescue dog from Dogs 4 Rescue in Manchester. This was back in February 2020. I wanted a dog but wouldn't entertain the idea of getting one from a breeder. Even before my time at Street Hearts, I knew that there were so many unwanted dogs, and so paying exorbitant prices for one that's bred particularly for that reason wasn't for me.

Bryn is part Staffie cross, possibly mixed with a bit of whippet. His story was that he had been at the pound for a week and so, as an unclaimed dog, his time was up. He was about to be put to sleep when Dogs 4 Rescue took him in and I took him from there. I'll never know his background, but I suspect that he was used for breeding and then dumped. Fostering him was the turning point for me. He's a brilliant dog and now lives out in Bulgaria with me, where he gets to run around all day with the dozens of other Street Hearts dogs.

I got to hear about Street Hearts through Dogs 4 Rescue, and once I came out to Bulgaria, I saw for myself the incredible, relentless work Emma, Anthony and the rest of the team do. Two weeks into my six-week volunteer stint, they offered me a full-time, paid, live-in job.

It's certainly a contrast to my last career. I had worked free-lance on adverts, music videos, launches of new football kits, that kind of thing. It was great fun and I really enjoyed it, but I knew that it wasn't going to be a path I wanted to go down for decades to come. I wanted something else from life. I've certainly got that, and I love it.

I had one hesitation about taking the job at Street Hearts – how would society view this way of life? It's anything but the norm. The expectation is that everyone should get a 9 to 5 job, work five days a week, buy a house and get a mortgage. I wasn't setting out to do any of that, yet I knew that this was the right thing for me. I completely love doing something that really matters. I get to be a part of something worthwhile, live in the beautiful Bulgarian mountains and have a healthy lifestyle. This is my second home, and even the bad days are worthwhile because of the difference we make to so many dogs' lives. It's what I want to do and, since coming back, I've not thought twice.

My first day here was spent being shown around and I was in awe of the shelter. It was a memorable day, seeing the dogs in their runs and being out on the pack walk with them, watching how everything fits together and being a part of their typical routine.

Day two, however, was quite the contrast. Emma had arranged for me to go and watch neutering at the vet's. I witnessed Dimitar, our local vet, perform the operations and found the whole thing very interesting. Afterwards, I stepped outside for a few minutes and saw a local man walk down the short hill and into the vet's car park. Although I'm not medically qualified to comment, I think it's fair to say that he might have had some mental health issues. He was pushing a shopping trolley on wheels with a box on the top. Inside the box was a tiny puppy, about eight weeks old. She absolutely stank; she was wet and covered in her own bodily fluids and clearly in a lot of pain.

The man explained to the vet that he had seen someone in a car purposely run over the puppy and her brother. The other puppy had died. The puppy he had brought to the vet had a gaping hole in her stomach and, as was later established when she was examined and X-rayed, a broken pelvis on one side and a broken hip on the other. The smell coming from her stomach was like rotting flesh. This man had picked her up and kept her at home for two days before taking her to seek veterinary care. He appeared to lack the insight to realise that she was at death's door and infected.

Dimitar took her in to his practice, disinfected her insides and stitched up her stomach. That was as much as we could do at that time as she was so tiny.

It wasn't long before Emma and Anthony arrived at the vet's. They had been to the nearby wood yard speaking to the premises' owners, whose dog had had an unwanted litter of puppies.

The wood yard owners said that they would allow the mum to be neutered, if, in exchange for letting this happen, Street Hearts took the four puppies off their hands. As Anthony started to pick them up, one had screamed. The protective mum, keen to stop anything happening to her offspring, charged at Anthony and savaged his leg. They had managed to get the four surrendered puppies and the overly aggressive mum into the back of the Toyota truck; meanwhile, Anthony's leg was dripping with blood.

I'd just watched Dimitar neuter three puppies, I was carrying a cardboard box with a puppy someone had deliberately run over with their car and was about to die, and Anthony's leg had been mauled in the process of saving four other superfluous puppies so that their mum could be stopped from having any more unwanted dogs. It's an overview of how crazy and over-whelming it can be here. In only a few hours, it summed up Bulgaria and the problems we encounter.

We called the pup Lola and I took her home. I fostered her, and she developed into the most incredible, funny character. It was a joy to watch her flourish into such a wonderful dog. She grew in strength, weighing in at around 27 kg at her peak. Her story has many highs and lows – and, ultimately, the lowest of lows. She had so many operations and went through so much. I tried to house-train her, but she was in so much pain, it was so difficult for her. I also attempted to lead train and that was incredibly hard too. How do you lead train a puppy that can't really walk? She needed physio to help her leg after every operation.

Tragically, the injuries she sustained at such a young age, and the damage caused to her back and hips from overstraining throughout her entire short life, meant that we had to say good-bye to Lola when she was around a year and a half. She is a dog that I'll never forget. If I hadn't worked so hard with Lola to rehabilitate her, I would never have got to see past her injuries to the magnificent dog she truly was.

One of the fantastic things about this job is the feedback we get when a dog we've rehomed has made their life with a family in their home. That means that we've done a good job and the family is committed too. It's a perfect happy ending, especially knowing where the dog has come from. A great example of this is the story of Ariel.

Ariel had a bad start in life: her mum was a street dog who had puppies, one of them getting run over by a car – sadly, it's a common theme. A woman found her and brought her to the shelter in a cardboard Ariel detergent box. Ariel had terrible mange and vomited a ridiculous amount of bugs. She must have been eating them to stay alive and, at that time, we didn't think that she had much longer left to live. As the weeks went on and she grew stronger and bigger, we noticed that she had some quirky behaviours, such as being scared of visitors. We wanted to start the process of looking for adopters for her. Because of her background and quirks, we knew that this wasn't totally without risk, but we're always open and transparent with anyone looking to take one of our dogs. If there are any issues, we work through them, and this is what happened to Ariel.

Happily, when Ariel was ready, she had a lovely home waiting and I was able to go on the next transportation run with Anthony, taking her to her new home, along with nineteen other lucky dogs. Ariel was nervous when she got there and met her adoptive family, yet she quickly bonded with their other Street Hearts dog and their two young sons, and she's slotted in with the entire household. She has the nicest life and sleeps curled up on their beds.

I've always wanted to work with rescue dogs, but particularly specialising in overseas dogs. I know that there's money in dog training, however, my heart is in helping dogs with a really poor start in life and liaising with adopters to get the best from the dogs they've chosen. I absolutely adore working here at Street Hearts, although I'm not sure that I'd want to run my own shelter.

Apart from the type of tasks you'd expect anyone working with dogs to carry out, such as walking, feeding, grooming and clearing up after them, I make some of the potential adoption calls to the UK. Emma and I tend to split them between us; sometimes we make them together, it very much depends.

We always want to see the people applying for our dogs, so it's always a video call where we ask a lot of questions. It's important that we make sure everyone in the family is on board with it and we're matching the right dog to the right family. Every single adult in the house has to want the dog and we have to make sure that the environment is suitable for her or him. It's not that we won't let single people in flats adopt a dog, but we owe it to the dogs to make sure the conditions are suitable. If we don't, we're setting them up for a fall. We don't want that, and it causes heartbreak for the adopters, as well as confusing the dog, potentially regressing it back beyond where it started.

Once someone has taken on a Street Hearts dog, it never ends there. We support people – and the dogs – throughout. For a transport trip of twenty dogs, I probably receive about four calls for aftercare advice. It's usually just a quick call, someone wanting some ongoing support. Only recently, someone who had adopted one of our dogs a year ago contacted me for some advice and I was able to help them. Sometimes I have six people email me in a day, and then I might not get a call for a week. Whatever the dog, situation or adopter, I can and always will help.

The most frequent problem I'm contacted about? It's overwhelming the dogs too quickly. It either makes them reactive or shutdown and nervous. If they're exposed to too many people or places too quickly, it's bound to happen. We always tell people not to walk the dog for three days after the trip. Puppies especially should always be exposed to bite-sized chunks of an unfamiliar environment, and it should be controlled. People often flood their new dog and it simply can't keep up. The dog will end up barking, or too boisterous, as it's overwhelmed by it all.

There aren't any particular problems associated with specific breeds. The nature of what we do means that our dogs aren't pure bred; they often come from guarding or hunting breeds, so they have a high prey drive or, sometimes, bad recall. If someone tells us that their dog is guarding, for example, we'll tell them how to stop that behaviour. It may be that the dog is an adult and has over five years of previous less-than-ideal habits, so we can explain how to stop the dog from constantly alerting them to visitors.

Some of my work involves outreach work. We go into towns and villages to capture stray dogs and to do whatever we can. I can't stress enough how much I love living here, but I think it's important to explain how Bulgarians can sometimes behave. They will crowd round us and discuss what's happening, sometimes talking loudly; some are abrupt with us and talk about us as if we're not there. Others will tell us that we're doing an excellent job and, while Bulgarians won't actually thank you – it's one of their traits not to do so – they will tell us, 'Well done.' That's their version of gratitude.

39.

More Changes Are Coming

Emma – Now

Anthony and I have always faced the low points together, ready to meet whatever life throws our way. But the news that our good friend Jane Duberley had cancer was devastating beyond words. The very least we could do for our friend was ask her to move into our bungalow where I would revisit my nursing days and do everything that I could for her. It was such a privilege to be with her in her final days. Her beloved daft dog Teddy stayed by her side, literally, sleeping on her bed.

At 2 a.m. one freezing cold February morning, I heard Teddy howl. The sound carried across the courtyard to our farmhouse bedroom, the sound jolting me awake. Then every dog in the Street Hearts shelter began to howl. Every single one of them. I knew, I just knew that Jane had gone. The human part of me didn't want to accept it, the professional part of me knew it was true and the part that made me adore my friend meant I had to face it. With heavy heart, I went to check on her.

Teddy is the most wonderful dog, but I don't think he'll ever get over Jane's death. Animals definitely feel loss.

There are still dozens of dogs to be cared for. Teddy being one of many, for now anyway. We've had the very happy news that someone who adopted Winnie, a blind dog, from us last year, has opened his home to Teddy. Teddy doesn't know it yet, but his life is about to change for the better.

Then, as I tackle today's rota of tasks, Luke, our three-legged labrador cross, starts to chase Teddy, who – despite being of a comparable size and build and in possession of all his legs – demonstrates he clearly isn't in the mood today. Tiny Little Blackie with the big personality shows her displeasure at the rudeness of it all. Even before dozens of the others start to bark at the sound of a vehicle coming up the steep, bumpy track, I know we are about to have an unexpected visitor.

I pick my way through the gaggle of dogs. I make it across my once-beautiful garden, the spot I had once earmarked for paying guests to practice their Downward Dogs in my yoga retreat. Now its grass is a little on the patchy side from the constant canine scratching and digging, flowers a dim and distant memory and my cherry tree long gone, once the dogs decided it was no longer needed. I wouldn't have it any other way – most of the time – apart from the days where I think, 'what on earth have I done?' Although, with yoga would have come people and loads of hassle, so that probably would have been overrated as well ...

The dogs start to bark, and we all turn towards the gate at the edge of the property. Anthony and Lauren have only just reached England, and Pauline and Tatiana are out walking the puppies. Our other Bulgarian team member, Lucy, hasn't told me about anyone coming to see her, so I'm intrigued, to say the least, to see who's on their way up the track.

The sound I can hear, alongside the chorus of dogs who have all joined in now that one of them has been alerted to a visitor, is someone heading here with a purpose. Nobody just passes through, especially as Anthony went off on one at the merest suggestion that the stone track would be owned by the municipality. I smile at the thought of his annoyance. I do miss him when he's on a transport run.

Experience tells me the noise of the vehicle isn't indicating the wanton abandonment of a once-owned dog either. The ones we discover tied to our gates are always left in the dead of night. We learnt the hard way that our dogs are quieter if they're tucked up for the night before we turn in for the evening. That ensures they don't make much noise until we let them out in the morning. That's when we find the often terrified and always bewildered animal tethered to the gate by the person who was supposed to look after it. At least these are the people who take them somewhere to be cared for, and not shot or poisoned when the animal is of no further use to them.

I hurry through the door set into our high solid wooden gates. I step outside, not hanging around; something everyone learns very quickly here. Dally in the doorway and at least one dog will take advantage of your dawdling. I'm outside in front of our main property, our volunteers' house set back across the path, and I'm momentarily stunned at the sight that greets me.

I stand at the edge of the single track outside our gate; the sunlight temporarily impairing my vision as it glares against the taxi's windows. A young woman in her twenties, cradling a black and white puppy, pushes open the door and climbs out of the back seat. She tries to speak to me in Bulgarian, until her voice catches, and she starts to cry. A man of similar age gets out of the other side of the Kia and walks round, talking to her, comforting her and trying to explain to me at the same time why they've taken a six-hour round taxi journey from Sofia to Street Hearts. We speak in Bulgarian, and he tells me they didn't want to entrust their puppy to anywhere else in Bulgaria than our shelter. They've heard about us, researched us, and know that some of the state-run municipality shelters leave a lot to be desired.

They tell the taxi driver to wait – not that there's much else he can do – and ask me to take the puppy. The woman tells me that when it was obvious they were going to struggle to keep what would become a fully grown Karakachan dog in an apartment, they knew that giving her up was the kindest option. It's clear how much she loves the dog.

The last thing we need in our shelter is another dog but turning her away isn't an option. I lift the puppy from the sobbing woman's arms and lead them inside to complete the paperwork. Fortunately, one member of our team who hasn't gone on the transport run in the bus or out walking the puppies is Lucy. Being Bulgarian, plus fantastic at her job, having Lucy around will help no end.

I call her up on the walkie-talkie and the four of us introduce Nora, the inquisitive puppy, to one hundred of her newest friends.

40.

Here Comes the Autobahn

Anthony – Now

After a reasonable night's sleep on the bus we crack on with the morning schedule. Once we've taken care of the walking, feeding, cleaning and group messages, we're ready to set off towards the Czechia–Germany border.

This border is soft, meaning it should be straightforward. However, it's one I always approach with trepidation. Our Bulgarian-registered bus usually draws the attention of the German police, meaning inevitable delays. Still, it's quicker than driving around the entire country. Such a phenomenal detour would clock up too many miles and take too much time. Still, at least the police, unlike some members of the German public, don't swear and shout abuse at us. This is the only country it happens in, and as soon as I speak to them in English and they realise that I'm not Bulgarian, the verbal barrage stops. Strange, isn't it? The police are equally flummoxed when I produce a British passport; they aren't quite sure how to process the information. A German police officer once told me that he stopped me because of the Bulgarian number plates. He then asked, 'Do you have any secrets?' After asking me a couple of times, he resorted to making smoking actions with his hand. 'You mean cigarettes?' I said. 'No, I don't have any.' He said, 'Well, you should, it's good business! Buy cheap in Bulgaria and sell in England.' Another remarkable encounter with the law.

If the police officers who stop me are reasonable and interested, I'll show them the documents so they know what they're looking for in future. I'm trying to educate them to show what is and isn't an illegal transport run. Sometimes the police photograph the documents so that they know what's correct and what isn't. Some even ask me for photos with the van and dogs. One police officer asked if he could hold the dogs and started to tell me about his own dogs, so it's not always a bad experience. It's easy to remember the negative ones and not recall the good ones. Although, now I think about it, that was in Belgium with a Belgian policeman, not in Germany at all.

We cross the border without any problems and head towards to the west of Frankfurt. Our next pit stop is a place we've paused at on many of the journeys, some with fewer incidents than others. Lauren reminds me of the charmer we got acquainted with on our last trip who shouted and swore at us as we got out of the bus. I tell Lauren that in the unlikely event we bump into him, I'll simply remind him that what we're doing is perfectly legal. And, like last time our paths crossed, he should use his smartphone to scan the QR codes on the side of the Street Hearts' van and come back to me when he's done so. It was Lauren's first time having someone rant at her on the journey, so she was a little more taken aback by it than I was.

Would Germans approach a truck driver with chickens or calves and have the same attitude they frequently have towards us?

Still, in the interests of balance, some remarkable and hard-working Germans have volunteered at our shelter over the years and made a positive and important difference to the dogs' welfare and rehabilitation. I don't want you to think that all the hostility and yelling from passing members of the public has given me an attitude.

To be fair to Angry Man, he did have the courtesy to return to the bus twenty minutes later and admit that he now realised that what we were doing was all above board and official. He thought that we were Bulgarian, which we get a lot because the vans are Bulgarian-registered with Bulgarian and English sign writing. Even so, it was an improvement on another expedition through Germany, when three cars blocked us in. It does pay to be vigilant, so I expect that not much goes on here that isn't noticed by the authorities. And I should also add that many, many Germans have adopted Street Hearts dogs from us and other rescue shelters. As I said, I like to be fair and balanced in my recounting of my experience in Germany.

Back to the dogs.

I've done the journey across Europe so many times now. Emma and I started our own transportation runs in October 2018, shortly after we got our shelter licence. The first two trips were in our old bus, Frieda, which now has a new lease of life as our chicken house, and the remainder of the trips have been in one of the newer buses, most of the funding for which came from our army of incredible supporters. Emma used to accompany me on the trips, although she tends to stay at the shelter these days. Mostly Lauren comes with me or sometimes Lucy. The journeys aren't for the faint-hearted and can surprise people at how exhausting they are. We can't miss the Eurotunnel crossing, so any delay has to be made up somewhere along the route. Lucy and I once had seven and a half hours to catch up. We didn't reach Czechia until 3 a.m. There are added concerns that something might go wrong with the buses, which is why it's important to keep the vehicles well maintained.

On three occasions, our patron Kate travelled out to Bulgaria, worked with us at the shelter and then travelled back with me in the bus. Kate is a remarkable person to have on the trips. She is great at controlling the dogs, walking them and updating our progress on social media for the eager adopters waiting in the UK. On our second trip to England, I dropped Kate at a hotel in Nuremberg, where she was meeting some friends. She got out of the bus and I helped her with her luggage to the hotel door. It was late in the evening and raining hard, so I wasted little time in getting back into the bus. There was a vehicle parked at the rear quarter of the bus, and through the dark, I couldn't see clearly and assumed it was a taxi dropping someone off. The vehicle didn't leave but slowly moved backwards and forwards. All the while it was being driven in this strange manner, I sat in the driver's seat and waited. I couldn't pull away, solely because of the vehicle alongside mine. It took so long, I realised that I couldn't go anywhere, so I found my food in the glove compartment and ate my sandwich. If nothing else, I took the positive from the scenario that I wouldn't have to stop again for a meal break.

The vehicle was still there when I'd finished eating so I jumped out to speak to the driver and suddenly saw flashing lights – it was the police. One of the officers got out of the police car and told me, 'You can't park there.' I told him that the only reason I was parked outside the hotel was because I had dropped someone off and now his police car was blocking me in. He said he was going to give me a ticket for parking in the drop-off zone. Again, I remonstrated that the only reason I was still there was because he had blocked me in. His answer to that was that I was sitting in the passenger seat, so I couldn't have tried to drive away. I pointed out that his observation skills weren't fully developed as the van was right-hand drive. He then said, 'And it's illegal to eat when driving.'

To say I was losing my patience by now wouldn't be an exaggeration. Despite repeatedly telling him that I wasn't driving and eating, but blocked in by his car so I couldn't go anywhere, he wouldn't back down. A crowd had started to gather. The concierge stepped in to join my side of the heated debate and meanwhile, Kate had seen that I was having problems and came back outside to join me. When I seemed less than elated at the prospect of taking the officer's ticket, he raised the tariff. His revised offer was to arrest me. There was no possible way that I could be arrested when I had twenty dogs in the van.

I had little choice but to take it. When I returned to Bulgaria, one of the volunteers we had living with us in the shelter at the time, Noah, who happened to be German, paid the fine online and registered a complaint on my behalf. I never received any response.

Lauren and I have a small bet, a bar of chocolate is the wager, each of us guessing how many times we're going to get stopped by the German police before the border. As I drive us across into Belgium, I head for Liège, towards our final overnight stop before England. Again, we feed and walk the dogs and then, before turning in for the night, I present Lauren with a large bar of chocolate. She had 'two' in the sweepstake, while I had 'four'. I'm pleased to say it was actually only once this time.

41.

The Full Force of the Law

Emma – Then – August 2022

I had high hopes for 2022. The previous year had been the usual mixed bag: happily, 160 dogs had been adopted from our shelter and had started their well-deserved new lives. Sadly, Stefi our shelter manager, who had taken over from Dan when he returned to England, had left at the end of the year and returned home to Germany. We were extremely sad to see her go but saw the same potential in Lauren when she volunteered here. We offered Lauren the job and so we went seamlessly from one superb member of staff to another. Once again, our supporters continued to amaze us with purchase after purchase from our Amazon Wishlist, dog sponsorship, contributions towards veterinary costs and endless fundraising. Anj, who had adopted two dogs from us, donated her Gucci watch for auction to raise money, making a whopping £592.50 for the shelter. There was also an increase in the number of local people who brought their dogs forward to have them neutered at Dimitar's veterinary practice.

Battersea Dogs and Cats Home once again made a massive difference to our education programme. At the beginning of the year we received a project development continuation grant from this prestigious and iconic organisation. This helped us to teach children and young adults the importance of dog and animal welfare. It allowed us to work alongside the ABC Language Centre and to plan more education and open days, all absolutely essential. Another huge boost was that it allowed the continual employment of our community outreach staff, all such good news for the dogs in the Dryanovo area.

Since July of this year, we had another new team member, Tatiana O'Mahony. Tatiana is originally from Russia and had lived in England for many years, before moving to Bulgaria in 2015. She heard about us from Street Hearts' team member Pauline Trent and started working for us four to five days per week. We were going from strength to strength.

Then, as if the balance was tipped the other way, trouble drove straight through the fencing onto our private land – the land we pay the municipality 760 leva (about £380) to use.

Totally unaware at the time, I was dealing with a precarious situation of my own. I had just caught Big Lad with a bone that he managed to find somewhere. I got it away from him and shoved it into my inside pocket. He got his head up my jacket as he tried to get at the bone. I was very well aware that his jaws were next to my vital organs, stomach and chest. I knew that even after all this time, he could be so difficult to manage with anything that he regarded as high value, such as a bone. If he ever got out of his comfort zone, that was when he'd start snapping so we understood that we had to be really cautious. As I knew to be confident and calm with him, it ended well, which is more than I could say for what was unfolding in the field a couple of minutes' walk from where I stood, soothing Big Lad.

The second I heard Lucy shout for help over the walkie-talkie, I grabbed my mobile phone and ran out of the farmhouse, up the incline to the field where she was. In February 2022, Lauren had been walking her dog Bryn and one of our rescue puppies on our land. A man who had previously been spotted skulking around in the bushes walked onto our private land and threatened to kill the dogs. He then started to kick and beat them with sticks. We called the police, the case went to Gabrovo court, where the man received a warning and threat of a fine if he ever harmed our dogs again. This resulted in another inspection at our shelter from the authorities. Now, he was back, along with his son.

I kept it together as I dialled 112 and told the operator I needed the police to come out, we had been targeted and attacked again. Lucy and the dogs were unharmed, but the damage to the fence and tracks through the grass was evident. I was shaking with rage by the time the police came.

I would love to tell you the police took the matter seriously, but no, they interviewed all of us as if we were the criminals. I was so upset that, once more, here I was trying to do the right thing and clear up someone else's problem, and all the while we were being targeted and attacked. What was more, incredibly, we were being made to feel that we were in the wrong. As if what had happened to Lucy wasn't bad enough, we were being dismissed by the police. It made me so upset, I started to cry. That made it worse. It really knocked the wind out of the police officers; their shoulders dropped, along with their faces. The massive physical change in them was something else. It seemed that they were as used to women crying in front of them as they were to women shouting at them.

It still didn't stop them from giving Lucy a warning not to harass this man in public – the same man who had driven through a fence to get onto our field and at our dogs. If there was a logic to this, I couldn't tell you what it was. This incident and all of the previous incidents have occurred on our private property, not in public.

We were told to expect another inspection, only this time from a higher authority. We weren't entirely sure why being the victim of crime resulted in inspection after inspection. We felt as though we were being held to account for why someone else was attacking us.

Not to be deterred, and still determined to do everything officially, on the same day, I made a full complaint to the police. I detailed the harassment we experienced, plus the threat to our staff, volunteers and dogs. I promise to let you know if I ever receive a response.

To be clear, we have never initiated any contact with these people. If we see them in the village, we stay clear. When we care for and walk the dogs, it is on our owned or rented property. To avoid any behaviour on our part which could be construed as antagonistic, we never walk the dogs during hunting days, so we don't interfere with the hunters' hobby. They have absolutely no reason to come onto our property or have anything to do with our work. We also have an agreement with the local farm who allow us to walk our dogs on their adjacent property.

258

Following this last incident, Anthony wrote a statement and Teddy (Teodora) Marinova, who worked at Dimitar's veterinary practice before she joined our team, translated it. We drove to the police station and gave it to a police officer. This time, the anger was back and I lost my temper. I said to the police officer, 'We're doing this for the good of the village and these people are trying to stop us. They are the problem, not us.' He told me to calm down – does that ever work? – and said that he would really back us and appreciated all that we did.

With the constant struggles, you may be forgiven for thinking we were losing hope. Not at all. After what had happened with Benny No Neck, I felt that we had won the battle. The municipality had always been behind us but we were even stronger than ever. As well as their unwavering support, what helped us to turn a corner was running the education days. The children like what we do so the older people put up with us.

I've got thick skin and I'm resilient, however, when you're passionate about something that you love and want to make a difference – and we do it for the dogs, not for me – and someone criticises you, it stings. Social media can be an enemy sometimes. If we share something, we're open to criticism. Social media makes the world go round: it's where people choose to adopt, support us, donate to us, fund us, but it's a difficult world to be in. But, truth be told, social media made me start to feel a bit ill. Luckily we've got Laura Norrey now and she takes a lot of it on. Our paths crossed when Laura saw our adoption advertisement for Lidi, a sweet ginger street dog we'd seen wandering around a supermarket car park begging for food. She followed us to our car, so we brought her back to the shelter and named her

Lidi from Lidl. Laura joined the team in March 2021 and since day one has done a remarkable amount of work for us. If she didn't manage most of our social media content, I don't think I could have continued. Especially in the early days, people were so quick to criticise. We share a lot and we're open and transparent. Sadly, that makes us a target.

Laura's spare bedroom is always brimming with dog food, treats, worming tablets, dog beds, disinfectant, brooms, mops, buckets – everything and anything our amazing supporters have bought online for us between trips, before Anthony brings it all back to the shelter on the return leg of the transportation run.

Laura takes so much pressure off us by keeping on top of our social media throughout the day and co-ordinating adoptions, running and maintaining the WhatsApp groups and chats for the transportation runs and has, on more than one occasion, fostered dogs for us. This has been either when things haven't worked out with the new adopter or there's a brief period of time before the adopter can take the dog. If there's a day or two overlap between Anthony getting to England and, for example, a family coming back from a holiday, rather than postpone the dog's arrival to the next transport run, Laura steps in and helps us all out by looking after the dog. We don't know what we'd do without her.

Laura Norrey, adoption co-ordinator, social media manager, administrator, fosterer, general all-round saviour

My husband and I had a much-adored border collie, Chuck, who died in June 2019. Naturally, we were devastated and when we were ready to have another dog in our lives, we tried a couple of

UK rescue shelters, but things didn't work out and they weren't a good match for us. Eventually we found Street Hearts through Dogs 4 Rescue in Manchester, saw gorgeous Lidi on their website and fell in love with her. I instantly knew that she was the dog for me. I showed her photo to my husband, not that I remember giving him much option, and I told him that we were going to adopt her.

Lidi arrived in our Derbyshire home in June 2020 and I couldn't be without her. She gave me a sense of purpose when I was feeling at a loss. The pandemic meant that I, along with pretty much everyone else in the UK, was stuck at home. I'd also been made redundant from my job and, in general, things felt overwhelming. However, Lidi made me laugh and smile every day, gave me a reason to get up in the morning, and brought me joy and happiness beyond measure. She also helped my husband and I to heal after losing our wonderful Chuck.

Lidi helped me in more ways than simply being an amazing dog and companion: she brought Street Hearts into my life. I met Anthony on collection day when I picked her up and we got chatting about all sorts, including work. In March 2021, I started to do some online voluntary work for Street Hearts, helping Emma reply to all of the messages and emails. After a week, they offered me a full-time job as their social media manager and adoption coordinator. I have a masters in animal behaviour and have always wanted to work with animals. To have the opportunity to do such a brilliant job was something I was never going to pass up.

As well as the social media and adoption tasks I do as part of my role, I'm always pleased to be in a position to foster dogs for

Street Hearts too. Lidi is a fantastic foster sibling to the thirteen Street Hearts short-term buddies she's helped me to look after. I had eleven of them in 2022. No matter how many, it's always sad to see them leave: Kiera was the first one I ever fostered and when, after three months, she left for the West Country, I cried.

The adoption process has changed over the years, as there were failures in the early days when Street Hearts didn't handle everything themselves, before they were arranging the adoptions and taking the dogs to the UK. It's very rigorous now and everything goes through us. It starts with someone filling out an online adoption form on the Street Hearts website. Emma and I review it to see if it gets through to the next stage. If it's too vague, we don't pursue it. That does happen from time to time, but most people provide sufficient detail for us to gauge whether they are serious adopters. The form asks for a few details about the person looking to adopt, as well as what their ideal dog would be – male or female, puppy or adult and the type of energy level they would want in a dog. We're trying to match the ideal dog with the ideal home, so we need to know about everyone in the house, especially young children. We ask about the activity levels in the house, as some dogs need someone around most of the time, others, as you would expect, require more attention. We also ask potential adopters to provide reference contact details, which is something I follow up too, once the rest of the process is completed.

I do quite a lot of the first adoption interviews, which can last one to two hours and can be intense, so I don't make more than two calls a day. I speak to all of the adults in the house; in case one person isn't keen, it saves time further down the line. We need everyone in the house to want to adopt one of our dogs. We ask what their experience of previous pets has been and whether they have had an overseas rescue before. Street Hearts dogs haven't all been used to being in a house and haven't had the same level of exposure to vacuum cleaners, motorbikes, television – the kind of everyday things that UK dogs would be more familiar with. We emphasise that adopters shouldn't walk the dogs for the first three days and then to start off slowly to stop them being overwhelmed. We are always up front with any issues, behavioural or physical, that a dog might have. It's not in our interests to keep these things under wraps, so Emma or Lauren will always inform the adopters of any concerns.

Once all of the questions are asked, we introduce the dogs. We save the best until last, especially as there's no point in doing it before then. As soon as the camera is on the dog, everyone is far too distracted to talk about work and school schedules.

We never shy away from telling the would-be adopters about the hard work of having a dog, especially a rescue. People sometimes forget it's very hard work. There is a settling-in period, adjustments, sleepless nights with puppies and the chewing. We don't see it as bad if people drop out at this stage as it's better to do it now than later when the dog has travelled for days to another country.

We ask for a WhatsApp video of the downstairs of the house, garden – if there is one – the boundaries and front of the house. We need to make sure there are no gaps in the fences. Providing everything looks acceptable to all parties, I then send out the paperwork along with a contract. The adopters also receive guidance packs. The pack provides links to videos to help them with crate training and other queries or concerns they may have. They are always welcome to call me, and often do. I'm glad to help. There is also a pre-adoption online seminar with Kate Lamb which takes about one and a half hours. She covers how to get a dog to bond with you and your children, and a host of other useful information.

As soon as Emma and Anthony have the transport trip dates, I then send the transport forms. Three weeks prior to the dog leaving the shelter, we take the rest of the adoption fee, the deposit having been paid when the adoption is confirmed as going ahead. The whole process is very streamlined and works well, although we understand that it can be tough on people if they aren't suitable for a Street Hearts dog. Since September 2022, we have been so focused on how to get things right, we've had very few failed adoptions.

I have great fun setting up the adoption trip WhatsApp group. I add each of the adopters to it, along with Anthony, Emma and Lauren, and monitor the messages. After Lauren posts photos of each dog along with its neck, chest and back measurements and height – vital for buying crates and harnesses – the next step is Emma telling us that the state vet has looked through the passports and other documents and the dogs will be leaving in the morning. Then I let everyone know about Kate's online training and that their dogs' health certificates and information have all been submitted to DEFRA, allowing them legal travel to the UK. I follow up with an email link to the pre-recorded version of Kate's presentation so they can watch it back, if need be. In the excitement of their new dog only days away, it's understandable if they need to watch it again.

Sadly, there have been instances where someone has adopted and subsequently their circumstances have altered for the worse. Occasionally, someone has been taken seriously ill, and understandably, they aren't in a position to keep the dog. Whatever the circumstances, we'll step in and do what we can.

These days, it's usually Anthony who travels over with the dogs, although Emma does sometimes make the trip too. It's always great to see him, especially as he takes the plethora of Amazon Wishlist merchandise from my house with him. For a couple of days, at least, I can use the spare bedroom again. Before long, there's a wealth of shelter essentials stacked around the walls sent by generous supporters.

I travelled out to Street Hearts in 2022, spending a month there, and it was the best experience ever in my life. Ideally, I would love to go out there once or twice a year, other commitments allowing.

42.

Brace Yourself

Anthony – Now

Chocolate devoured – Lauren shared it with me after all – I drive us across the German border into Belgium. Liège is our final overnight stop before England. Lauren and I need to be up at 4 a.m. to get the walks and feeding taken care of for a really early start. We need to be the other side of Brussels as soon as we possibly can as the traffic is always terrible. It's worse than London, so I always make sure that the cut-off point for getting away is 6.20 a.m. at the latest.

By now, the journey is starting to take its toll on us. We know that the end is in sight, but these trips require stamina. No one enjoys them, although I find that I can tolerate them more than most, largely because I have to. The last one Emma and I did together was in November 2022. Like most people, she doesn't relish the idea of eight nights in a van sleeping in a narrow bunk bed. She didn't enjoy a frosty night's sleep in Czechia when there was snow on the ground either, although she always loved to see the adopters pick up their newest family member. Lucy has done four or five trips, including one in January 2023 where she met up with Millie, the dog she found and brought to the shelter in 2020. Millie now lives in Cheshire and it was clear as she ran towards Lucy, jumping all over her and licking her, that she recognised her. During Dan's time with us, he did three or so, and Lauren has done more than her fair share. Hers sometimes ending with a stay in England visiting her family before she travels home. The final leg of her journey back to us at Street Hearts is in a taxi from Sofia airport, our trusted taxi driver and friend of ten years Viktor Ivanov at the wheel. Viktor has been driving the Street Hearts' team, our family, friends, guests and volunteers from the airport and back for the last decade. It's always a load off our minds to know someone trustworthy and reliable will be there for us at the end of a long journey. Still, the final stretch of our long journey to England is getting closer.

Between Belgium and France, we sometimes have to stop at the border. This has mostly been the case since Covid, but nothing compares to the Channel Tunnel. We have about another 200 miles to build ourselves up to this, the most gruelling part of the journey, chiefly because of the paperwork post Brexit. At least once we make it through, we can get the dogs somewhere they can properly let off steam and wear themselves out.

The chat between Lauren and me inevitably turns to the lives our former street dogs have in front of them. Although it was before Lauren's time with us at Street Hearts, I can't help thinking about so many of the dogs, such as Rufus who lives with Karen Croft in Yorkshire, Phoebe with Lisa Haslinger in Vienna and Bubbles who went to live in Kent with Michelle Harris and Dan Harding and their family. The list of over 1,400 dogs we have rehomed and who have taken this journey across Europe is far too long to mention. Then there are the ones like Big Lad who we can't rehome and live out their days with us. They are the really lucky ones.

With a sense of dread, I drive up to the Channel Tunnel check-in area, ready to explain all over again what paperwork I have to someone who, more often than not, doesn't really understand what it is they're looking at. At least the dogs are quiet.

For a number of years, before and after Brexit, we have seen a lot of large vans full of people, travelling from Eastern Europe to the UK to work. I know that England and other countries need migrant workers, and I have absolutely no problem with anyone going to another country for a better way of life. After all, it's exactly what Emma and I did. I also know that some people are forced, or at the very least coerced, into doing something that they may not want to do, so my next observation is purely that, and based on what I've seen, not the reasons, financial or otherwise, behind it. On more than one occasion at the tunnel, we have seen people jump out of the vans with a puppy, usually a tiny puppy that was far too young to be away from its mother. I've watched puppies get carried through security and passport control where the migrant worker passed the dog off as their pet. Their pet that has travelled in a box, the outsides drenched in what I could only guess was dog urine. I fully understand that a migrant worker's wages would be hugely supplemented by bringing a dog to the UK to be sold on. At maybe £500 per dog, it is a good return for the risk involved for bringing them in illegally. Perhaps what I've witnessed has been carried out under duress. It's not the migrants themselves I take issue with, it's the checks that should be in place to stop this. I appreciate the difficulty in proving that puppies carried in this manner aren't pets, but would you allow your own dog to travel in a saturated wooden box? We have gone to great lengths to make sure the dogs we bring to the UK are walked frequently and don't sit unnecessarily in their own squalor and filth. There are many other reputable rehoming charities from all across Europe who also do it the right way. Unfortunately, there are some immoral and illegal actions by a few that leaves a dark cloud over *all* foreign dog importations.

I have been through the Channel Tunnel on sixty or so Street Hearts' transport runs, and I have never seen a DEFRA representative present. If we can see that the puppy isn't the person's pet and there is a likelihood that it's being taken through to sell, then DEFRA must be able to see that too. Or, of course, they would be able to see it for themselves if they were there.

In 2022, there was a hold on dogs coming over from Romania, Ukraine and Poland. So many people went to Ukraine to bring dogs over to the UK and took them to the UK without the correct paperwork. Last year, each time I drove up to the Channel Tunnel, there were thirty or forty vans from all over Europe (some from the UK) all bringing dogs into the UK. As someone who wants dogs to be cared for and looked after, and who spends all of my time trying to ensure that happens, I absolutely appreciate why there was a blanket ban on dog importation in the countries bordering Ukraine. Fortunately for us, Bulgaria wasn't affected, so we could carry on.

It's brilliant for the dogs who come to the UK and have a new home; it's why Street Hearts exist. The problems arise when it isn't done properly, and this applies to UK charities as well as European ones. That's what might one day bring about an overall ban on bringing foreign dogs to the UK, not the charities who are completing their legal and moral obligations.

As things currently stand, it's legal for five dogs to travel into the country per vehicle. Battersea and other large organisations have tried without success to have a new animal welfare bill introduced that would reduce the number to three per vehicle. For unscrupulous dog vendors, all it takes is someone getting five dogs microchipped and then registered in their name. They simply go to the tunnel and present them as their own dogs. They could be pregnant, and there are no restrictions on them being neutered.

Because we travel through the tunnel for commercial reasons, no one scans the dogs. I don't know why this isn't done, but I have seen some of the dogs coming through from parts of Europe, and they are semi-feral. No one wants to get them out of the cage because everyone is scared of what the dog might do. I would scan every one of my dogs without hesitation or issue. If the dog is too volatile to be scanned, then it shouldn't be coming into the country.

A blanket ban on all foreign dogs will stop everyone bringing in dogs for adoption, including us. It is not the solution. There are uninsured drivers in England. What do you do? Ban everyone from driving? Although I can see and fear a blanket ban on foreign dog adoptions happening, it won't only stop the poor practices which are allowed to go unchecked, it will mean a certain death for all street dogs. It would undoubtedly bring an end to Street Hearts. We know that we can't neuter and release the dogs – they end up being poisoned. We need to educate people more than anything else so that the solution is no unwanted dogs on the streets in the first place. If we can't ensure the message spreads throughout Bulgaria before time runs out, it will be too late to save any more street dogs.

Now it's my turn to drive the van forward to the booth. The last words I'm expecting to hear today from the Border Force Officer who glares at my van are, 'You shouldn't be doing this. There are enough dogs in England already.'

Welcome home.

43.

Gostilitsa, Again

Lauren Hoodless, shelter manager

Every day at Street Hearts makes me feel so blessed that I've been fortunate enough to spend time surrounded by dogs. After my initial six weeks of volunteering here was up and Emma and Anthony had offered me a full-time job, I went back to the UK, worked in some kennels for a few months and then, in November 2021, drove back to Bulgaria with Bryn at my side. I used to go back to England once every two months or so for four or five days. However, now I spend about a third of my time there and the rest here in Bulgaria. To keep my training and knowledge refreshed, I completed a Level 3 Institute of Modern Dog Trainers qualification while I've been here in Bulgaria, as well as taking a one-day dog first aid course in Manchester. It's about managing my time: there's always so much going on here, but that will never change. We respond to every call and alert we receive, and some, naturally, stick in my mind and, I don't doubt, won't ever leave me.

Lucy and I responded to a call about a dog that had been spotted in the nearby village of Gostilitsa. We drove over to

where she was last seen and it wasn't long before we saw a pitiful
bitch scavenging along the roadside. She was in a bad condition
and full of milk. We couldn't simply take her with us; wherever
her puppies were, they wouldn't survive without her. We put a
lead on her and she took us straight to a fountain where she
drank a lot of water. She then led us to a farm towards a man
working in a field, someone we assumed was the landowner. The
dog was wagging her tail at him, leading us to believe that it was
his dog.

After a brief discussion – Lucy translating – he told us that he
didn't know where the puppies were on the farm, but if we
managed to find them, we could take them. He said that there
had been more puppies, but whenever one died, the mum would
remove the live ones to another location. He claimed not to
know how many there had originally been or where the dead
ones were. It was an absolutely horrendous experience being on
that farm. As he walked us across his land, it smelt of death. I
saw skeletal calves standing in mud and excrement. It's the
saddest sight I've ever seen, and I've seen a few during my time
here.

The farmer allowed us to take the female dogs for neutering,
although he wouldn't let us take the males. The dog took us
straight to where she had left her two puppies.

Lucy explained to him why the mum was so poorly and he
said we could take the puppies as he didn't want them but he
wouldn't give the dog up permanently. He said that she was a
hunting dog and he was reluctant to let her go. After some
persuasion, he said that we could take her for treatment, but he
wanted her back. We nursed her back to a decent weight, took

her to the vet for inoculations and neutering, and saw a huge improvement in her.

In the meantime, the farmer repeatedly asked for his hunting dog back. Even though it was the last thing we wanted to do, we had little choice but to return her to him. As we handed her back, we gave him plenty of advice – much of it translated by Lucy – about the need to give all of the dogs food, water and shelter. It's fair to say that when we returned her, I would have said that she was in full health.

Tragically, it didn't end there. A couple of months later, we went back to see if there were any more females that needed neutering. We've learnt very quickly that the only way to keep the street dogs under control is to neuter as young as we possibly can. We asked the farmer about the hunting dog that we'd got back to full health and where she was. He told us that he hadn't seen her for months. It seemed strange, as this was a dog that we offered to take off his hands and he insisted he wanted back. Despite this, he allowed us to walk around the farm again, the stench of dying animals still thick in the air.

We got to where we had last seen the dog and all that we found was the skull of a dog that had been chained to a post.

We'll never know if it was the dog we'd tried to save or another one. All I can say is that this was such a low point for me; I simply couldn't make sense of it.

We reported the farm and the farmer for the state of the animals. The place was, at best, alarming. The police, food standards agency and municipality all came out and inspected the premises, and all claimed that the animals had water and shelter so there was nothing they could do. To make matters worse – if you can imagine them being any worse – the farmer was the same person who had kept six dogs chained up in a house in Gostilitsa. One had starved to death, one had gone mad from being on the brink of starvation and the others, including Renée and Phoebe, were rescued by Anthony and Emma. This was the man who had been banned from keeping animals.

It affected me so much: it's not rational here at times, so much so that I can't make sense of it. We're supposed to be protecting these animals, and yet we proved nothing. These people don't care and they're not held accountable. How is this right?

At least the gorgeous puppies of that hunting dog we rescued, the one who was never seen again after we returned her, are now living in the UK. That kind of scenario is why, thankfully, even the grim days have a glimmer of hope.

44.

There's Always Hope

Emma – Now

The day is starting to warm up by the time I head back to the shelter from the pack walk. Some of the dogs left before me and are waiting at the gate for me to let them in, some have been let in by Pauline or Tatiana and many are wandering along behind me or chasing each other through the trees. They always come back – every dog wants a nice warm bed and a full tummy.

Speaking of full tummies, Del Boy, one of our long-term Golden Oldies, appears and eyes me warily. Del Boy along with Rodney, Marlene and the gone-yet-never-forgotten Raquel were rescued from little more than a dilapidated shed in the woods. Still, our racy golden girl Bonnie has struck up a relationship with Del Boy since Roshy's passing. Bonnie tends to get into bed with him, and that's something in itself. Del Boy hates most other dogs and has the same feeling towards most humans, the exception being Anthony. Del Boy can't be rehomed for that reason, so he'll live out his days with us, along with Bonnie – if she feels like tolerating him, obviously. He stares at me, realises

I don't have any treats and takes himself back off again. Del Boy is content with his life – his ever-growing waistline is proof of that.

When it's hot and heading towards summer, it's always a good idea to get the dogs out for their walk as early as possible. There are plenty of shaded areas for them when the sun is beating down, even if the humans don't get to cool off.

There's always enough to do, but I'm especially pleased that we'll be welcoming visitors into the shelter in a few days' time. Anthony is on his way back to Bulgaria from the transport run, and so he should be here in plenty of time to help set up for the education day. We also have to get prepared for the Street Hearts stall at the town fair in a fortnight. We know the value of speaking to people and showing them how incredible dogs are. Valeri and Nellie adopted Ellie the former Bus Stop Dog after seeing for themselves how incredible she was. If we can manage to open people's eyes to the joy of a dog being your companion and friend, perhaps we can afford to pause and take a breath of fresh Bulgarian air. Our first educational trip was for twenty children who came with their teachers. I cried when I first saw the children's faces gazing at the dogs in total wonderment. It was as if we'd gone from helping the animals to helping the people.

On a subsequent educational day, the grandfather of one of the attendees adopted one of our dogs after hearing so much about the positive parts of having a dog. It's still unusual, although not completely unheard of, for Bulgarians to adopt dogs. It's imperative that we have somewhere that local children and community members can gather to learn about dog care and welfare, as well as responsible ownership. The last thing we ever want is for people to adopt when they don't understand how to look after the animals.

We would love to have dog and puppy training classes at our shelter. Other than raising some funds it would, above all, be reaffirming that many people here do love their pets and want the best for them. There is a pet shop in Gabrovo where customers often enquire about dog training, but there is no one in the area who can do it. Right now, we don't have the time or the resources to fill this gap, although it would be a welcome addition if we could train our team to do it. The education centre would be my ideal place for it, although, once again, another obstacle is where we are located. People here don't allow their dog in their cars, so they would be hard pushed to get them up here.

The educational days we run stopped some of the resistance we were getting. Children here are everything, so in turn it changed the older generation's approach. Those who attended went back to the community centre and, through Antoinetta Stavreva, word spread about what we were doing. In the past, there had been what I hoped were jokes from some who wondered what we were doing with so many dogs, and perhaps if we were eating them.

We have arranged six education days at the time of writing. Some of the children are scared of dogs. It's only natural that some would be afraid; here, dogs are culturally used to guard the house, warn the occupants and ultimately bite intruders. If there's an element of fear amongst some, we can go into the schools and talk to them without them being petrified of the one thing we're trying to introduce them to. We work with the ABC Language Centre on an educational programme for children. It's wonderful to see them engaged and learning about dogs and looking after them.

Each of the educational days we have here can cater for twenty to thirty children. We had twenty-five here from a kindergarten class, and I have to say it was chaotic. The teachers are the ones who orchestrate it and have to endure the melee. It's such a superb day when everyone arrives, especially in the warm summer months.

In December 2022, children from a local school came to the shelter to drop off Christmas presents. The dogs were given plenty of toys and 80 kg of dry dog food. We were so grateful to them and for their enthusiasm and engagement throughout the day. It was the first time that children from this particular local school had visited us, and we hope to have them back again soon. It was also the first time that we had been given Christmas gifts for the dogs, making it a very special visit indeed.

Once again, much of this is down to our amazing supporters who donated nearly £17,000 via JustGiving. This raised 75 per cent of what we needed for the education centre, volunteer accommodation and dog rehabilitation space. When we set up the volunteer apartment, we knew the importance of the dogs being comfortable in a home. Many of them have only lived outside chained up or on the streets. We knew how difficult it would be for the dogs to spend days in a crate travelling to their new homes and then being traumatised at being shut inside a house. In the last three years, over 100 dogs have spent time in the volunteer accommodation to get them used to being in a home and around people, sleeping in their crates under the same roof as the humans.

As well as Lucy, we also have another Bulgarian member of the team. Teddy (Teodora) Marinova joined the team in June 2023, having worked as the veterinary assistant for Dimitar in Dryanovo. Teddy had been working there for almost three years, after returning from Norway. She initially left Bulgaria to study in Northern Norway for a year, while she completed her BA in hotel management and marketing. After working there for another eight years or so, she wanted to come home. Luckily for Street Hearts, Teddy having worked for Dimitar, along with her love of animals and unwavering support of us, meant that it was a natural progression for her to join us. To have another team member, especially a Bulgarian who is known and admired around the area, is a coup for us. From the very start, Teddy has given talks in Sofia to municipality representatives, spent time with children on our educational days, represented us at Tryavna fair and appeared in endless short media clips asking Bulgarians to care for and neuter their dogs. We don't know where we would be without her.

Even more exciting news is that Lucy was stopped in the town yesterday when she took one of the puppies on his socialisation and familiarisation walk. A young Bulgarian couple asked her how they went about adopting a dog. They had seen some photos of Nora, fallen in love with her and wanted to come and see her. They'll be here any minute and from the sounds of it, they seem to have fallen hard for her. Could this be the younger generation of Dryanovo helping us turn a corner? Nora was only dropped here by her former owners days ago. They had taken the six-hour round trip from the capital city to make sure she was cared for, and now she has the glimmer of a furever home.

I have no regrets about anything that Anthony and I have done here. Anything that hasn't gone particularly well, I'd look at and learn from it. The only thing I'd change is realising the importance of education earlier on. We didn't have the resources or the money to get involved in educating people when the shelter was in its infancy, or in fact, before we even became a shelter. If anyone was going to set up and do what we're doing, I would tell them to get on board early with the local community; I'm still not where I want to be with that. I think there are still a lot of people who don't know about us or our work and I'd like to change that. The open days at the shelter are imminent, so that's a waymarker. We need people to start adopting from us directly, here in Dryanovo, and taking responsibility for the problem in their area and becoming more involved. That's the only thing that I'd change.

Anthony and I long for Street Hearts to break the cycle of unwanted dogs and discarded pets thrown away like rubbish. We dare to hope that a new home for Nora is the start of a process that will hopefully render us redundant.

Until then, we have dogs to walk and puppies to feed.

Acknowledgments

Emma and Anthony would firstly like to thank our families and friends for supporting us, encouraging us to be ourselves, and follow our dreams.

Thank you to Lisa Cutts who listened to our stories for literally months on end and made sense of them for this book! We are eternally grateful for your enthusiasm and dedication to making this book become a reality.

Thank you to Joanna, our agent from Hardman and Swainson, who read our book and wanted to achieve publication. A big thank you to the team at Harper North who wanted to publish *Street Hearts* and tell our story.

A huge thank you to our supporters and adopters who keep us going. Without your donations and encouragement, we couldn't save the lives of so many dogs. Our adopters have not only saved the life of their own Street Heart, but they have also created a space in the shelter for another dog in need.

Many thanks to Dryanovo Municipality and Dr Vasil Petrov

(BABH) for their help and support in ensuring our transport and shelter management complies with EU and UK animal welfare laws. We could not have done this without you all.

Thank you to Battersea Academy for their incredible support. Your education programme and grants process have made us what we are today.

Thank you to Jane and Dave Harrison, our trustees, who have helped us with accounting and been at our side since day one, despite your own challenges.

We thank our wonderful team, past and present, who have each brought valuable knowledge and experience. For us, you are like family and much loved.

Thank you to everyone who has contributed to our book. You all have a very special place in our hearts.

Finally, we would like to thank all of the dogs who have entered our lives and the impact they have had on us.

THANK YOU EVERYONE.

www.streetheartbg.com

Do follow our social media channels for up-to-date news:

Facebook – facebook.com/StreetHeartsBG
Instagram – @streetheartsbg
TikTok – @streetheartsbg
X (formerly twitter) – @streetheartsbg
YouTube – @streetheartsbulgaria
LinkedIn – linkedin.com/in/streetheartsbg

Harper
North

Book Credits

HarperNorth would like to thank the following staff
and contributors for their involvement in
making this book a reality:

Fionnuala Barrett

Samuel Birkett

Peter Borcsok

Ciara Briggs

Katie Buckley

Sarah Burke

Fiona Cooper

Alan Cracknell

Jonathan de Peyer

Anna Derkacz

Tom Dunstan

Kate Elton

Sarah Emsley

Simon Gerratt

Lydia Grainge

Monica Green

Natassa Hadjinicolaou

Megan Jones

Jean-Marie Kelly

Taslima Khatun

Holly Macdonald

Petra Moll

Alice Murphy-Pyle

Adam Murray

Genevieve Pegg

Natasha Photiou

Emma Rogers

Florence Shepherd

Eleanor Slater

Emma Sullivan

Katrina Troy

For more unmissable reads,
sign up to the HarperNorth newsletter at
www.harpernorth.co.uk

or find us on Twitter at
@HarperNorthUK

Harper
North